CW01645144

To Ray

Many Happy Returns

on your '100th' birthday

Very best wishes

Nick

God Bless.

The Revival

This book is a work of non-fiction. While every effort has been made to ensure accuracy, the author accepts no responsibility for any errors or omissions. The views expressed are those of the author.

First Edition – 2025
Printed in the United Kingdom
www.nickfletcherpublishing.co.uk

ISBN: 978-1-9191948-1-3

Cover design: Nick Fletcher

Disclaimer

This book is a work of non-fiction, based on the author's personal experiences, opinions, and research. While every effort has been made to ensure accuracy, some details may be subject to interpretation or change over time. All facts have been checked against reliable sources at the time of writing; however, to preserve the flow of the book, no footnotes have been included.

The views expressed are the author's own and are not intended to malign any religion, ethnic group, organisation, or individual.

To my wife, family and friends for their love and support and to everyone who still believes Britain can be great again.

Foreword

Over the past ten years, I've watched our country and much of the Western world seemingly lose its grip on common sense.

My time in Parliament was a steep learning curve. As Tony Blair once admitted, it was only when he was leaving that he truly felt equipped for the job. I can relate.

Since leaving the House of Commons, things have only worsened. This book has been written in the summer of 2025, one year into a new Labour government.

Many of the issues I address here are shaped by this moment, but many others do not change from one century to the next. Unless we have a nation and leaders who understand the basics of a strong economy and the need for a grounding in Christianity, I believe many of these challenges will remain.

It's a book I hope many will read cover to cover, but it's also designed so readers can dip in and out, tackling one issue at a time. Each chapter addresses a topic that matters from today's hot debates to the deeper lessons I've learned as a Christian, a husband, a father, a son, a businessman, a landlord, and, more recently, as a Member of Parliament.

I hope you find it as useful to read as I've found it to write.

With my very best wishes,

Nick Fletcher

Preface

This book wasn't written with publishers in mind. It wasn't written to make money, go viral, or fit any trendy agenda. It was written because something is going badly wrong in Britain and I couldn't stay silent.

After spending time in Westminster and many more years in the real world, running a business, raising a family, and trying to live as a decent man in modern Britain I came to a simple conclusion: common sense has left the building.

Too often, ordinary people are shut out of the debate. They're labelled bigots, dinosaurs, or conspiracy theorists for asking fair questions. Meanwhile, those in power keep pushing the same broken ideas, pretending everything's fine. It isn't.

This book is for the people who see that. For those who've had enough of being talked down to. For those who love this country, who want to raise strong families, who believe in fairness, hard work, and truth and who feel increasingly like outsiders for holding those views.

Each chapter tackles one issue. Some are political. Some are cultural. Some are moral. I don't claim to have all the answers, but I do believe in speaking plainly and offering practical solutions. That's what this book is about.

Read it front to back. Or just dip into the chapters that interest you. Either way, I hope it makes you think and maybe even act. Because if we do nothing, we know where this ends. But if we speak up, stand firm, and hold the line, there's still time to turn things around and be part of a revival we desperately need.

Nick Fletcher
July 2025

About the Author

Nick Fletcher was born and raised in Armthorpe, Doncaster, and attended the local comprehensive school. Leaving at 15, he followed the path of many in his generation and began an apprenticeship. He trained as an electrician at the Plant in Doncaster, working on railway engines and cabins destined for London.

In 1994 he was made redundant. After three months of searching unsuccessfully for work, he took the plunge and became self-employed as an electrician a decision that proved wise, as did marrying his wife, Gail, in 1995.

Over the years his business, grew steadily. Now based in Harworth, it employs more than 20 staff. Nick and Gail live in Doncaster, and their two children are now grown up.

Politics had long been an interest. Nick became Chairman of Doncaster Conservatives and was later selected as the Conservative candidate for Don Valley in the 2019 General Election. The seat had been held by Labour since its creation. Against the odds, he won with a majority of 3,630.

As a backbench MP, Nick did not seek ministerial office. His priority was bringing prosperity back to Doncaster through building a strong local economy. He also set up a Role Models programme in local schools, producing a manual that was distributed in the community.

In Parliament, he chaired the All-Party Parliamentary Group on Issues Affecting Men and Boys, where he called for the creation of a Minister for Men and a Men's Health Strategy. He also served as a member of the Education Select Committee.

Since leaving Parliament, Nick has returned to his business, launched another enterprise, and written this book. He intends to write more in the future and perhaps, one day, return to Parliament.

Above all, Nick Fletcher is a Christian, a husband, a father, and a conservative who loves his country and wants to see its people thrive.

Contents

Family

Education & Technology

British Culture

Afterword

Politics

Politics shapes almost every part of our daily lives, from the taxes we pay, to the roads we drive on, to the laws we live under. Yet too often we treat it as something distant, complicated, or even irrelevant.

For many, the difference between local, regional, and national government has simply never been properly explained. Fewer still have been taught how decisions are made, where power really lies, or how their vote connects to change.

This section isn't here to tell you who to vote for. It's here to help you understand the system, the parties, and the people who operate it. To give you the knowledge and context you need to make an informed choice. Because an uninformed vote can have dire consequences.

These chapters may not offer all the solutions. Instead, they are about equipping you with the tools to recognise what's being promised, what's possible, and what's simply political spin.

If we want a revival. A genuine, lasting renewal of our country. It must be built on a foundation of knowledge. And that starts here.

Governance

"We do not have government by the majority. We have government by the majority who participate."
— Thomas Jefferson

As I pounded the streets on the final day of a recent Mayoral campaign, I knew I'd lost before the polling stations even opened. Why? Because my main opponent had gone into hiding, and Nigel Farage was busy campaigning on "stopping the boats" something the Mayor has absolutely no power to do. Many of the public simply didn't understand the role of the Mayor. Some thought they were voting for Farage. They weren't. Those who did understand had lost all interest in politics and weren't going to bother voting. And to be honest, I don't blame them. Nothing was working, and apathy hung heavy across the borough.

As predicted, I lost the election. The outcome? With only 30% of Doncaster turning out to vote. As Thomas Jefferson said: "We do not have government by the majority. We have government by the majority who participate."

A Reform council and a Labour Mayor were put in place, and Doncaster was effectively crippled for another four years. Why? Because the Mayor holds executive power, not the councillors. Most of the new councillors didn't understand that at the time. They do now.

Things need to change. My hope is that by understanding how power is structured from Prime Minister to parish council you'll not only take part but do so wisely. And take heart: even if your chosen candidate doesn't win, your vote still mattered.

Let's start at the top and work down. You may be surprised just how much power some councils have. But the "mother of all parliaments" is the House of Commons, so that's where we'll begin.

The country is split into 650 constituencies. Each one is represented by a Member of Parliament. At a general election, all parties select their candidates and campaign to get our vote. The candidate with the most votes wins and takes their seat in Parliament.

The leader of the party with the most MPs goes to Buckingham Palace and asks the King for permission to form a government. This is just a formality, but it must be done.

The leader then becomes the prime minister (PM) and appoints a government. They select MPs to become secretaries of state to run each department, and ministers to support them.

There are around 25 departments, though this can change over time. Some are larger than others and therefore have more Ministers.

The prime minister, secretaries of state, and ministers have two jobs. They continue to represent their constituencies as MPs, and they also run departments in line with the manifesto the PM campaigned on.

Some departments are huge. However, even the smallest employ many thousands, of civil servants based in London and across the country. Take the Department for Education, for example. It employs approximately 8,600 civil servants and that's not including teachers. These are big departments. I'd say too big. So would many others.

But here's the bizarre part: much of what happens in the day-to-day running of a school is decided by the principal of each individual school.

Many voters believe that structure, discipline, and homework policies can be changed by the secretary of state. But these are decided by the headteacher. Ministers are responsible for the curriculum, funding, the exam system, and teachers' pay. Under Conservative governments, much power has been passed to schools themselves, and you'll see that pattern repeated throughout this chapter.

Parliament may be the 'mother of all parliaments' but it's no longer where all the power lies.

Which brings us to backbench MPs. What can they do? Well, it depends on the quality of the MP. A backbencher has no executive power like a secretary of state, PM, or even a school head, but they do have a voice. And if used wisely, they can achieve much.

What about the parties that don't form the government? The largest of them becomes the Official Opposition. Every time the PM comes to the

House, whether for Prime Minister's Questions or to make a statement the Leader of the Opposition stands at the despatch box opposite.

The same applies to secretaries of state and ministers. Every time a government minister makes a statement, the opposition has a shadow Minister to challenge them.

Smaller parties don't have the same platform, although their leaders do get more chances to speak than backbench MPs, especially during Prime Minister's Questions (PMQs).

Whenever the PM wants to pass new legislation, it must be brought to the Commons, debated, and voted on. It then goes through multiple steps, including committees, back to the Commons, and then to the House of Lords before being ratified by the King. Again, just a formality, but it must happen.

So, as you can see from the school example, the Secretary of State can't control exactly how your child's school is run. But they can provide the funding to ensure teachers are paid and that what children are taught meets the needs of the country. How it's taught is down to the head.

I can't move on from Westminster without saying a word about the House of Lords.

The Lords are often the target of criticism, mainly because they're not elected. A small number, 92, are hereditary peers, remaining from an older system. Others, it's true, are there through cronyism. But many are there on merit, based on the work they've done throughout their lives, which has been recognised with a peerage.

As much as they may disagree with the government of the day, they can't stop legislation outright, because they're not elected. The real power in Westminster lies with the House of Commons.
So, what is the Lords' role?

When a piece of legislation has passed through the Commons and all the committee stages, it goes to the Lords. They debate it too, often more thoroughly than the Commons. The Lords get a bad rap for turning up, claiming expenses, and leaving again. But the ones I've known are often much older than me and many sit in the chamber until the early hours.

You might have seen them nodding off now and again and yes, it's not a good look. But at 80 years old, at 2 a.m., I can see myself doing the same.

I often think of the Lords as someone checking your homework before handing it in. I've never been in government, but I can understand how frustrating it must be for ministers when the Lords try to amend their work. Still, whatever others may say, I believe many of them work hard. And many have real-life experience that some MPs simply don't.

Maybe it's the selection process that needs reform, not the abolition of the Lords altogether. We'll have to see what happens.

There has definitely been a shift to move power away from Westminster. I don't always agree with it. Devolution has been one of the biggest political changes of the past 20 years. Scotland, for example, now makes many of its own decisions and continues to push for more powers to control its own affairs.

I won't go into detail here, because it's a vast and complex subject. But at present, it doesn't appear to be working. The devolved governments seem more focused on picking fights with Westminster than delivering better outcomes for their people.

Another shift of power has been to the creation of combined authorities, and this is the next layer of governance I want to cover. The country is being gradually divided into city regions or combined authorities. These areas are led by mayors and they're beginning to wield real power.

I can only speak for South Yorkshire, but here, the Mayor has responsibility for skills, transport, business growth, housing and infrastructure, and the police as Police and Crime Commissioner (PCC). He also has around 200 staff to help deliver his plans.

Funding settlements from government, such as Gainshare or the City Region Sustainable Transport Settlement give these mayors large sums to invest in their region.

I've seen firsthand the problems that come with giving this much power to one individual especially when the public doesn't fully understand how it works. This confusion is common across every layer of governance.

For example, a combined authority mayor has power over major local issues, but many people still think that power and money remain in Parliament.

A case in point is the closure of Doncaster Sheffield Airport. I repeatedly lobbied the Mayor of South Yorkshire to support our airport, but he kept blaming the government. Yet the money now being used to potentially save the airport can only be signed off by that Mayor.

And here lies the problem: when a decision goes right, the Mayor takes all the credit. When it goes wrong, he blames Westminster. And he gets away with it, because people don't know where power lies. You do now!

Next, we come to local councils. These can be unitary or district councils. The current government wants to transition all councils to unitary status, so we'll focus on those.

Each council is divided into wards. Depending on the size of the ward, it may elect two or three councillors. Once again, parties put forward candidates, and they campaign for our votes.

When the votes are counted, the party with the most seats takes control of the council. Each party has a leader, who, like a Prime Minister, forms a cabinet and appoints committee chairs.

Most councils have civic mayors, the ones in robes and chains but these have no power. Their role is ceremonial: promoting and celebrating local events and individuals.

However, some areas do have elected mayors who do hold real power. These individuals are elected separately and can, with the help of their cabinet, make decisions for their entire area without needing approval from the rest of the council, except for major issues such as budgets.

Just to loop back: combined authority mayors work alongside multiple councils in their region. They regularly meet with council leaders or mayors who lobby the combined authority mayor for money and share ideas.

Councils themselves handle a long list of vital local responsibilities: bin collections, adult and children's social care, potholes, and even some schools (called maintained schools). They also shape the vision for their area, oversee local markets, housing, planning, highways, the list goes on.

They receive funding from four main sources: central government grants, combined authority allocations (if they are part of one), and council tax. They also raise income through business rates. Supplementary income can come from parking charges, planning fees, licensing, and other local services. Councils manage substantial amounts of public money, often hundreds of millions of pounds.

Like all levels of government, councils have statutory duties they must meet. But what makes the biggest difference is vision, work ethic, and leadership.

A socialist leader (and as you'll read later, socialism never works), with no vision and a weak work ethic will only deliver poor outcomes. You'll see them take credit when things go right and blame central government when things go wrong. It's a tired pattern.

It takes real backbone to say no to the endless stream of demands. And it takes real intelligence and ambition to say yes to the right ones and push forward with sound ideas. But when you're a socialist at heart, that vision is often doomed from the start. Because socialism simply doesn't work.

Let me give you an example of where government funding can be catastrophically misspent. The Conservative government, much to my dismay (yes, capitalists can get it wrong too) allowed local authorities to bid for money to install cycle lanes.

I understand we want cleaner air. I get that. I also understand the desire for a healthier population. But should it come at the cost of the entire economy? I'm not convinced.

Either way, cycle lanes became the fashionable solution, so councils across the country started digging up perfectly good roads and pavements to install them.

The result? Every main route into a city is now strangled. Roads are so narrow that ambulances can't pass in an emergency. You've probably seen the junctions where the cycle path and footpath have been raised or brightly painted. Drivers are now expected to give way to both cyclists and pedestrians, even those walking on the road. Everyone has right of way except the poor driver, who pays for everything.

It now appears that every footpath in the country that was once for pedestrians is fair game for cyclists. And the worst part? In many city centres, the people using these cycle lanes are often undesirables in balaclavas, running drugs across town. Are our taxes now supporting county lines?

When you challenge a ward councillor or a mayor, it's never their fault. It's always central government. The reality, it's usually both. But one thing's for sure; few wanted these cycle lanes, and even fewer are using them.

Finally, we have parish or town councils. Not every area has them, but they can be created if enough local people lobby their ward councillors and a vote supports the idea.
These councils aren't supposed to be political (though, many are). Members should be residents who put themselves forward for election.

Each council sets its own size. If the number of candidates matches or is fewer than the number required, they're elected uncontested. If more people stand than there are seats, a local vote takes place.

The mayor of a town or parish council is chosen by the councillors, not the public.

These councils receive money from a precept; a charge added to your council tax bill. They may also raise money through things such as renting out community halls or car parks. This money should be used for the good of the local area.

Meetings are held regularly, and the public has a chance to speak at the start of each one. Even here, you can have problems too.

Mayors who want to raise and spend a budget of £2 million instead of £1 million will always find ways to tax local people. Tax so they can have personal assistants. Tax so they can decorate the town with furniture no one asked for. Tax to put on events nobody wants to celebrate. No, even at the most local level, politics can have a detrimental or positive effect on our lives.

Now to the question does your vote matter? I often hear, especially in Labour heartlands: "What's the point? Labour always win." But recent elections have shown that's no longer guaranteed.

And even if your candidate doesn't win, your vote still makes a difference. Why? Because the narrower the gap between those elected and those not, the better politician you'll get. A leader with a 70% majority might take their position for granted. A leader with a 2% lead won't. They'll have to work harder to keep their place and to earn your trust. So yes, your vote always matters.

So, there you have it. The tiers of power. The politics of blame. The hope that the right people are elected. And, hopefully, a clearer understanding of how much your vote matters.

Voting on national issues when choosing a mayor or a councillor can be disastrous. My advice: do your research. Look around your area. Vote for individuals based on what they've done (or not done) and what you believe they will (or won't) achieve.

Maybe the best way to decide is to look at your pay slip and council tax bill, see how much you're directly being taxed, and ask yourself: would you trust the person on the ballot paper with your country, your town, your children's future and your money?

Whoever you decide to vote for, the most important thing is to use your vote.

It matters more than you think.

The Main Parties

Conservatives, Labour, and the Liberal Democrats. For most of our lifetimes, it has really only been two main parties that shaped government: the Conservatives and Labour.

But times are changing. The Liberal Democrats are making something of a comeback and Reform has now entered the arena. Is this just a protest party, a flash in the pan? The polls suggest otherwise. Time will tell.

Before we go any further, let's be clear on something. In simple terms, the left favours equality, redistribution, and state intervention. The right favours freedom, individual responsibility, and limited government. Most parties shift over time, but understanding those basics helps when trying to work out where people and policies sit.

The Conservatives are, or at least are supposed to be, a right-of-centre party. But what does that mean? A right-wing party as stated above believes in individual freedom and responsibility and minimal state interference. But also, private property rights, meritocracy and competition.

It doesn't usually promise a utopia like socialism or communism. Instead, it assumes that free markets are the most effective and fair way to allocate resources. That means a state which taxes as little as possible, lets people run their own lives and finances, and trusts individuals to know what's best for themselves. A system that rewards hard work, encourages property ownership, and allows individuals to get ahead based on intelligence, effort, and skill.

In such a system, the state sticks to the essentials: defence, law and order, major infrastructure, health, and education, although even the last two could arguably be better run by the private sector.

From a personal perspective, as I'll explain further in the chapter on capitalism, I believe this is the system by which a country should be run. Why? Because it works. And why does it work? Because everyone has a stake in the game. People directly benefit from their own hard work. They have more money in their pockets to spend as they see fit. Services improve when shareholders expect a return on their investment. Large projects only get funded when they make economic sense, because it's someone's money on the line, and they have the option to invest it elsewhere.

Meritocracy means the best people get the top jobs, wealth is created, and we can all aim to own our own home. After all, an Englishman's home is his castle.

Labour, on the other hand, is the socialist party. Under Blair's New Labour, it shifted more towards the centre but under Starmer, it's firmly back to socialism. Left-wing ideology prioritises equality through redistribution. It favours collective ownership or state control of the means of production. It sounds nice in theory, fairness, equality, everyone looked after, but in practice, it never works.

Why? Because the people spending the money didn't earn it. And when they make mistakes, which they always do, it's not them who suffer. It's the taxpayer. Again. Taxes go up, not to fund success, but to cover failure.

Socialism doesn't promote accountability. It doesn't encourage excellence. Jobs go to those whose face fits, or to meet Diversity, Equality and Inclusion (DEI targets). People are promoted just to move them on, because no one has the backbone to say, "They're not good enough." There's no incentive to strive, because promotion or self-employment just means more tax and fewer rewards. In short, socialism kills ambition, wastes other people's money, and creates a bloated state led by the mediocre.

Liberalism often pretends to sit in the centre ground, but it doesn't. Traditionally, it's right-wing in many aspects. It values individual liberty, limited government, free markets, private property, and the rule of law. I want this book to be something anyone can pick up and use to grasp a subject, but I do have to reference some people many will not have heard of. I hadn't until well into my adult life. People such as Adam Smith and John Locke. Look them up. These were liberals, yes but also the clever minds behind the roots of capitalism and democracy.

But modern liberalism has shifted. It still talks about merit and freedom, but often prioritises progressive causes such as identity politics, group rights, and expanding state support, undermining the very values it once championed. While it may pretend be fiscally right-wing, it has socially drifted into left-wing territory. Nowadays, their MPs openly champion damaging ideologies, and as we'll see with other politicians, they use celebrity-style media tactics to get in front of the camera, whatever they look like. Most grown-ups think they look quite ridiculous, but it doesn't seem to deter them.

Now to the new kid on the block: Reform. A great name for a party. Its current leader, Nigel Farage, played the ace card by appearing on the reality TV show I'm a Celebrity. Proof, if ever it was needed, that politics is changing.

Reform have been very good at getting their message across, and I believe they've taken advantage of the fact that many people have never really had it explained where power lies. At recent local elections, for example, they campaigned on "stopping the boats," knowing full well that councillors have no control over immigration. That's misleading, to say the least.

But perhaps that reflects the state of the country. Many feel completely let down by the two main parties and think it can't get any worse. Trust me: if Reform were ever to win a majority with 360 brand new MPs; some of them suddenly responsible for roles such as Foreign Secretary, Chancellor, or Defence Secretary, all while still learning how to be an MP, it could get a whole lot worse.

That said, we shall see. They are a right-wing party, but they've spoken about nationalisation, a socialist concept. They only have four MPs at present, yet they're already split on assisted suicide, so there are clearly liberal elements too. Again, too early to tell.

One thing to watch, though, is the risk of vote splitting. If Reform continues to draw voters away from the Conservatives, it could hand Labour a majority by default. That's not strategy. That's self-sabotage. In our voting system, a party doesn't need to be universally popular; just unified.

Then there are the Greens. The title says it all: Net Zero and Liberal. What could go wrong? Well, pretty much everything. Luckily (or at least I believe it's lucky), they've never returned more than a handful of MPs, so they're not too much of a concern for now.

Still, it raises serious concerns. There are enough people in certain parts of the country willing to vote Green, knowing full well they'll never form a government.

In Scotland, the SNP has dominated in recent years, fuelled by nationalism and the independence movement. But their record in government has raised serious questions about public services, accountability, and financial management, proving that slogans don't substitute for sound policy. Nationalism might stir emotion, but it doesn't guarantee competence.

Regional parties like Plaid Cymru exist too but remain limited in their reach, often focused more on cultural identity and language preservation than national governance. Their appeal is strong in parts of Wales, but their broader influence remains minimal.

Brexit didn't just change our relationship with Europe; it reshaped our political loyalties. Traditional Labour voters in the Red Wall turned to the Conservatives in 2019, driven by frustration over immigration, globalism, and a lack of representation. Reform is now tapping into that same discontent. Voters who feel abandoned by the establishment are not necessarily turning left or right, they're turning away.

Politics today has become populist. Decisions are made based on media narratives, Twitter/X trends, and public moods. This is dangerous and sadly, many are falling for it, including the parties themselves.

When parties lose their identity, chase 'likes' on Facebook, follow trends, or bow to media pressure, they might gain some short-term support, but they lose their core principles. And when that happens, they start to look weak, make poor decisions, and lose the loyal support that once kept them in power.

The Conservatives under Thatcher brought smaller state, more personal responsibility, and enterprise. How did she do this? She cut taxes, sold off failing nationalised industries like British Telecom and British Gas, and reined in the trade unions. Council tenants were given the right to buy their homes. It was about ownership, enterprise, and letting people take charge of their own future. True Conservatism.

Under Tony Blair, Labour massively expanded the public sector. More civil servants, more targets, more middle managers. Spending on health and education rose sharply but so did bureaucracy. By the end of his time in office, one in five workers was employed by the state. It looked caring, but it created a bloated system with little accountability. Typical socialism.

Regardless of how you feel about either direction, both Blair and Thatcher stayed true to what their parties stood for. But that's what we're missing now.

The Conservatives have backed Net Zero ideology too hard and, desperate not to be seen as "the nasty party," have often ended up more socialist than conservative. Labour, meanwhile, have talked about cutting welfare and looking fiscally responsible, but they still can't shake the damage caused by their ideology. It all leads to voter confusion.

Many people still vote for the same party their parents did, but when those parties don't do what they're expected to, apathy kicks in. And rather than switch, many just stay home and don't vote at all, or, as we are seeing, switch to another party completely.

Maybe that's why Reform are doing so well. They only have four MPs, but their leader has made huge gains in the polls with populist soundbites and no real policy at present to back them up. But because they have no track record, there's been no drift and that gives people something to believe in. For now, at least.

Maybe that's all it takes: a break from the norm, some catchy slogans, a stint on a celebrity show, and an electorate tired of the main parties. And just like that, a new movement becomes a new government.

So that's left, right, and centre politics. And today, it's harder than ever to tell them apart.

My advice to any party: go back to your roots. Know what you stand for. Make sure your members understand your founding beliefs. Let every policy flow from your core principles. That way, there'll be less internal conflict, more stability, and the public will get what they voted for.

And to the voters: read the literature. Listen to news from a range of sources. Yes, mainstream media is biased, the BBC leans left, GB News leans right. Getting your news from one source is not the way forward if you want to make an educated choice.

The leader matters. If they are strong, they will surround themselves with the best people. If they are weak, they'll surround themselves with "yes" people. And if they try to please everyone, you'll never know where they stand. You will never like every policy a leader puts forward but choose a leader whose beliefs most closely reflect your own.

And look for the telltale signs of a weak leader. If a leader publicly claims that a woman can have a penis, I question their intelligence, courage, and honesty. I don't want someone like that leading our country. Do you?

A centre-right party, a great Conservative Party, with a strong leader who understands what conservatism is, and what it isn't, could do great things.

And when, as history shows, socialism, liberalism, and populism fail, perhaps the public will return to a true Conservative party. One that believes in Britain, believes in people, and makes our country once again the envy of the world.

Capitalism

"You don't get your dinner because someone was feeling generous. You get it because someone wanted to earn a living."

— Paraphrased from Adam Smith, The Wealth of Nations (1776)

As we saw in the last chapter, there are three main political agendas: capitalism, socialism, and liberalism.

Socialism and liberalism are often seen as the kinder choices. Socialism believes in making everyone equal. Liberalism believes everyone should be free to do as they please. Capitalism, on the other hand, often gets a bad rap, branded as uncaring and selfish.

But if you care to read on, I'll explain why the opposite is true.

At its heart, capitalism wants everyone to take responsibility for their own life, manage their own finances, and seek minimal help from the government. It encourages people to go out, take a risk, and make their own money.

As the quote above states: "You don't get your dinner because someone was feeling generous. You get it because someone wanted to earn a living." So, as you can see, capitalism is everywhere. Without it, we wouldn't have a high street. Would Henry Ford have ever invented the car?

Sadly, the world has been fed a very different message. Making money is seen as greedy. Profit is treated like a dirty word. Anyone who not only dares to have a go but succeeds is labelled selfish, crooked, or exploitative.

Films like *Wall Street*, where Michael Douglas's character famously declared "Greed is good," cemented this negative view of capitalism in the public imagination.

Too often, people confuse real capitalism with crony capitalism where favours, subsidies and loopholes replace fair competition. That's not capitalism, it's corruption dressed up as enterprise.

Socialists love the idea of everyone getting a fair shot, but don't you dare succeed. Because the moment you do, the politics of envy kicks in. Not only are you labelled all the above, but you're also taxed to the point where many start to think: what's the point?

It can already feel tough that the more you earn, the higher the rate you pay. But then you're taxed excessively on what you spend, just because someone decided you can "afford it." That's when entrepreneurs begin to ask the same question: what's the point? Let me give you an example.

I recently heard of an expensive car with road tax in excess of £5,000. That's right £5,000. They call it a green tax. The logic goes that if you can afford an £80,000 car, you can afford the tax. But that misses the point entirely.

Spend £80,000 on a car and you've already handed over more than £13,000 in VAT. To be in a position to afford it, as a company director you likely needed company profits of around £200,000. On that you'd pay about £50,000 in corporation tax. Then, when you take dividends, another £30–40,000 in dividend tax.

So, let's add it up: £50,000 in corporation tax, roughly £35,000 in dividend tax, £13,000 in VAT, and now £5,000 in road tax. That's over £100,000 in tax for one car. Still think dividends are too lightly taxed? What's the point?

This country needs entrepreneurs. People who are willing to step out, risk everything, money, time, reputation, on the hope of becoming their own boss. These wealth creators don't just pay income tax. They pay VAT, business rates, utilities, payroll tax, insurance… the list goes on. A director with the income in this example is probably contributing around £70,000 a year in additional taxes, on top of what they pay themselves.

If these people are so selfish and nasty, why are they funding so much of the country?

But ask yourself who's really contributing more to the country: the person sat at home on benefits, or the person working every hour under the sun, thinking constantly about their business, employing others, and putting hundreds of thousands a year back into the economy?

So why are the Conservatives who celebrate our entrepreneurs classed as the "nasty party"? Quite simply, there are more employees than employers.

Of course, there are bad employers out there. Not as many as people think these days, but they exist. Often, they get away with it by exploiting weaker individuals, those with health issues, poor references, or a lack of confidence. I'm sure I'd never have been exploited, but that's probably down to my upbringing. I was always taught, "I can, and I will" and that belief has served me well.

Not everyone has that confidence, though. So yes, we need some regulations. Without any, the drive of a strong boss could become too much for those with a different work ethic. A lesser work ethic is not a bad thing, if everyone was a workaholic entrepreneur, no one would be employed. We need people who are happy to do a good day's work, clock off at 5 p.m., and live a lifestyle that suits them.

But good employers, the ones who take the risk and put in the hours, shouldn't feel guilty for the rewards. Sadly, in this country, success isn't celebrated. It's resented. A complete contrast to places such as America, and even some African nations, where ambition is admired.

In fact, real capitalism depends on moral behaviour. In any functioning market, your reputation matters. You only succeed if people trust you, rate your work, and come back. That encourages honesty, reliability, and quality. It doesn't reward exploitation, it punishes it. It's no coincidence that every nation lifted out of poverty in the last 100 years has done it through capitalism, not socialism. Why? Because it works.

In comparison socialism feeds off envy, and with the help of unions, have pushed the message that all capitalists are bad. It's helped no one.

The relationship between employer and employee becomes strained. Taxes go up because politicians love to be seen taxing "the rich." And employment law becomes increasingly complex and expensive. More and more would-be entrepreneurs start thinking: what's the point?

And when they do, they stop hiring. Stop spending. Or they leave the country entirely.

Another thing that gets unfairly criticised is the zero-hours contract. "The Left" frames it as cruel and insecure. But for many people, students, part-timers, or semi-retired workers, it's exactly what they want. It gives them freedom. Flexibility. Choice. And for small businesses, it provides breathing room when work is unpredictable. Scrapping these contracts won't help workers, it will make them harder to hire in the first place.

A perfect example of this was when I worked in London. My wife came down to see me, and we decided to go for a walk. On our travels, we popped into a pub. There were only five or six people inside. I ordered our drinks and asked the manager, "Where is everyone?"

She said, "The train drivers are on strike. No one's in London. Tonight, we should have taken £3,500. We've taken £350. And I'm on my own; the young lad who was meant to come in had his shift cancelled."

Now, that's tough on the young lad. But at least the following week, he'd still have some hours. The alternative? A fixed contract. The business pays him to either stay at home or stand around at work doing nothing. Either way, the business takes a bigger hit and eventually shuts down.

Zero-hours contracts used just to dodge sick pay, pensions, and responsibility? I get why that's wrong, and I understand why there's been a push to stop that. But when employment law makes it so onerous to employ someone that small businesses stop hiring altogether, that helps no one.

My wife and I only had one drink. Who wants to sit in an empty pub? You see my point. So, what's the answer?

We need to educate people, especially the young, that capitalism is good. We need to show employees what employers do and go through. And we need a government that understands business. We should remind people that capitalism isn't just about business owners. Most workers are capitalists too, they have pensions invested in markets, own homes, start side businesses, or save for their future. Anyone who takes responsibility for their own money is part of the system. But all three are easier said than done.

Many educators hold progressive or socialist-leaning views, which can influence how they approach economic topics in the classroom. Without personal experience in entrepreneurship or running a business, some may lack a deep understanding of how capitalism functions in practice. As people age, their ideological positions often solidify, making it more difficult to persuade them with facts or alternative viewpoints, even when presented clearly.

I've learned this the hard way. No matter how clever someone is, if they believe you're earning more out of them than they are out of you, there's no way back. That belief, true or not, can create resentment. And resentment ends any chance of understanding.

And then there's government. For a secretary of state to stand up and say, "We're cutting taxes for the wealthy" is electoral suicide. To say, "The minimum wage is a flawed idea" same result. (There's a full chapter on that.)

Imagine a minister saying, "We're slashing benefits and increasing dividend allowances," or "We're removing unnecessary health and safety rules and trusting people to use common sense." That could be the end of their career.

So, we don't say these things. No matter how damaging the taxes. No matter how broken the wage system. Politicians of all stripes stand at the despatch box and proudly announce that "those with the broadest shoulders should carry the burden," while giving the lowest-paid a rise, paid for, of course, by someone else.

Worse still, governments and banks inflate away the value of money. They print, borrow, and spend and then blame businesses for rising prices. But it's not capitalism that causes inflation, it's often state interference. And the people hit hardest are the very one's socialism claims to protect.

The result? Appears to be a clear vendetta against capitalism. And it's visible in every part of the country.

You will have heard the phrase "trickle-down economics." Socialists love to mock it. They say it doesn't work. Technically, it means cutting taxes on businesses and high earners so they reinvest and create growth that "trickles down." Critics claim the rich just pocket the gains.

But when they're in power and a big business announces investment in Britain, they celebrate. Why? Because of the jobs it creates, from the six-figure CEO to the cleaner on minimum wage. That is trickle-down economics in action. It's employment based on skill, experience, and effort. It's how capitalism is supposed to work.

What's often missed is how competition, one of capitalism's core virtues, drives progress. It keeps prices fair, raises standards, and forces businesses to innovate. It's not greed that improves products; it's the fact someone else might do it better.

Socialists also love to say, "The rich get richer, and the poor get poorer." And oddly enough, I agree but not in the way they think.

Yes, the ultra-rich can get richer. And yes, the working poor can struggle. But that's usually when socialism crushes ambition. It makes people give up. It breeds failure.

With fewer people trying, we get fewer businesses. The few that survive grow into mega-corporations. And with fewer employers, there are fewer jobs. More people chasing fewer roles means wages fall. Those in work know they can be replaced at any time. The poor get poorer.

That's the irony. People think they're attacking capitalism by taxing and regulating small business to death but all they're doing is handing more power to the giants. I'm not defending multinationals dodging tax through offshore tricks. I'm defending the family-run firms, the builders, the tradesmen, the entrepreneurs who risk everything to create value and opportunity.

If we want to raise people up, we need to create an environment for many to grow not just a few. Make business easy. Make employment less bureaucratic. Encourage self-employment. Then more people become employers. And when lots of employers are chasing workers, wages go up, not down.

If we can teach this to our young people, if we can challenge those clinging to outdated socialist beliefs, we might one day see a government voted in with the courage to do the right thing. Not the popular thing. Not the vote-winning soundbite. The right thing.

Let me be clear: I'm not saying all rich people are virtuous or all poor people are lazy. There are bad employers, just as there are people who genuinely need support. But we've reached a point in Britain where those who take risks and build something from nothing are too often painted as villains. That mindset is toxic.

We need balance. We need some regulation, of course but we also need a cultural shift. One that respects effort, rewards success, and encourages more people to try. Because without those people, we don't have jobs, we don't have growth, and we don't have a future.

Capitalism works. Churchill put it very bluntly:

"The inherent vice of capitalism is the unequal sharing of blessings. The inherent virtue of socialism is the equal sharing of misery."

We must start explaining to the next generation how it works and begin celebrating it, not condemning it.

Democracy

"Democracy is the government of the people, by the people, for the people."

— Abraham Lincoln

This is the final chapter in my politics section though perhaps it should have come first. But now that you've read about the parties, what they stand for, and why I believe capitalism offers the best chance of success. I hope you're better equipped to make the right decision when you exercise your democratic right to vote.

One thing that's really depressed me in recent years is the low turnout at elections. I've touched already on voter apathy, why trust is low, why many people have given up, and why so many feel their vote doesn't matter. But here, I want to go a little deeper. Let's look at where this all began, and why your vote matters, win or lose.

Most people have heard of the Magna Carta. It was a document forced on King John by rebel barons in 1215. It didn't create democracy overnight, but it marked the beginning of something. Before that, the King was the law. And as with all absolute power, abuse followed.

King John was notorious for his cruelty and corruption. He taxed ordinary people to fund his foreign wars, often without success. The serfs, as the common folk were called, had no voice. They worked long hours, were treated terribly, and were taxed to the brink. If they couldn't pay, they were imprisoned. Even landowners weren't safe, if they didn't support the King, he could seize their land or even take their sons as hostages.
There's a saying: "absolute power corrupts absolutely", and King John proved it.

That's why the barons rebelled and forced him to sign the Magna Carta. It contained 63 clauses designed to limit his powers. He didn't stick to it, of course he appealed to the Pope, who annulled it, which sparked a civil war. But after John's death, his son reissued a revised version in 1217. The 1215 Magna Carta was more of a peace deal; the 1217 version laid legal foundations. It was also the first clear link between taxation and representation, a principle that echoed all the way to the American Revolution.

Over the centuries, more reforms came. Throughout the 18th and 19th centuries, voting rights slowly expanded first to working-class men, then to women. The Suffragettes are well known, and rightly so. Many of them were beaten and imprisoned. Some risked their lives. One died. All so women could vote.

That's why it's so disappointing to see how many don't bother. People today say, "What's the point?" But that kind of apathy just makes the problem worse. If we don't hold our politicians to account, why should they try harder? It becomes a downward spiral.

Some complain about the First Past the Post (FPTP) system, and I understand why. In the 2024 General Election, Labour won 34% of the vote and returned 411 MPs, while Reform UK won 14% and only returned 5. Under Proportional Representation (PR), Labour would have won around 221 seats and Reform around 91. So yes, PR looks fairer on paper. But it comes with big problems in practice.

Under most PR systems, parties submit a long list of candidates often over 300 names ranked in order. The higher up the list you are, the more likely you are to get a seat. It follows that if Reform UK took 14% of the vote under PR, the top 91 names on its list would take a seat in Parliament, regardless of where they're from or whether the local area voted for them.

That means the local link is broken. You could end up with an MP who has no connection to your community. Someone chosen by the party, not by you. Yes, that can happen under FPTP too, but at least under the current system your MP is elected directly by the people in that area.

PR also gives more power to small fringe parties. In theory, a party with just 1% of the national vote could get 6 or 7 MPs. Sounds fair, but in many countries these small parties end up holding the balance of power. They use it to extract deals and push through niche agendas. It's not about the public good; it's about political leverage.

And here's another issue: party lists are open to abuse. Who decides who makes it to the top of the list? Party insiders. Friends, donors, and those with the right connections often get priority. Good, local, honest candidates especially those without elite backgrounds, get pushed down the list.

In 2024, I visited Belgium, a country that uses PR. While being shown around their parliamentary chamber, we were told yet again, that the country was heading back to the polls. Why? Because small parties were holding up progress and the government couldn't get policy through. This isn't unusual there. In fact, Belgium once went 589 days without a proper government. That's the reality of PR constant coalition wrangling and political stalemate.

There are other systems too Alternative Vote, Single Transferable Vote, Mixed Member Proportional, and Two-Round Systems but most are just hybrids. Some are even more complex. Some reduce local accountability even further. All have flaws. There is no perfect system.

Some people look across the Atlantic and ask, "Why can't we be more like the USA?" They see Donald Trump a bold, combative figure, directly elected by the people and wonder why we can't vote for a Prime Minister the same way.

But the systems are completely different. The U.S. uses a presidential system, where the head of government (the President) is elected directly by the people through the Electoral College and is separate from Congress.

In the UK, we don't vote for a Prime Minister. We vote for a local MP. The leader of the winning party becomes Prime Minister. It's a parliamentary system, not a presidential one. Even if someone like Trump had massive public support here, they'd still need to become an MP, win their party's leadership, and lead that party to victory. Our system doesn't allow one person to run the country without first winning the support of both MPs and the public across the UK.

This can often make our Prime Minister appear weak. People think, "They're the Prime Minister they can do anything." But that's not true. They can, through their departments, introduce policy, but it must still be debated in Parliament and go through committee stages and the House of Lords. That's democracy at work. It takes time. You don't get strongman figures like Trump, but you do get accountability, checks and balances. It's not perfect, but it's democracy.

One area I do take issue with, though, is the amount of power now handed over to unelected bodies. We've seen it with devolution and combined authority mayors but at least those roles are elected. Quangos are not.

The term quango stands for Quasi-Autonomous Non-Governmental Organisation. In simple terms, these are public bodies funded by government but run independently of direct ministerial control.

And that's the problem. Quangos remove power from ministers and put it in the hands of unelected officials. This often means the minister the person you voted for, no longer has the power to change things. The body ends up doing as it pleases, while the electorate looks on, bewildered.

I don't agree with this situation. Decision-making must be in the hands of elected individuals, because if they get it wrong, the public can vote them out. That's how democracy should work.

Sadly, many of these quangos are now failing. The NHS, Ofsted, Ofcom, the Environment Agency the list goes on. And too often, ministers just use the chief executive officers (CEOs) of these bodies as punch bags, knowing full well they can't sack them or implement major changes.

This isn't just a bureaucratic flaw. It's a democratic one. And it's a problem we urgently need to address.

'We are where we are" as they say and as Churchill once said: "No one pretends that democracy is perfect or all-wise. Indeed, it has been said that democracy is the worst form of government, except for all those other forms that have been tried from time to time."

Some believe that changing the voting system will magically fix our politics. But the truth is, the problems run deeper.

We need good people standing for election. People who believe in the party they represent. People who are honest with voters. People who aren't just chasing a title, but who serve with integrity. And we need them to be accountable to their local communities, not protected by a party list.

I believe FPTP for all its faults, is the best way to achieve that.

But we, the public, have a role too. As we have seen earlier, whether your candidate choice wins or not, your vote still sends a message. If your MP knows they won narrowly or that a large number backed someone else that should drive them to work harder.

As with much of this book, one theme keeps repeating: personal responsibility.

Your vote matters. People lived responsible, moral, and upright lives before they ever had the right to vote but many were imprisoned, beaten, or even killed so that you could. Don't waste it.

Locally, I've said in many of my campaigns; I can be as visible as possible. I can knock on every door. I can answer every question. But I can't make you vote. That's down to you.

Final Word – Politics

Now you know the structure, the players, and the way power really works. You can't claim ignorance anymore and that's a good thing. Because informed citizens make better choices, and better choices are what this country desperately needs.

But politics isn't just about systems and parties; it's about people you, me, and the principles we live by. That's why the next section matters so much. Because without a moral compass, even the best political system will drift off course. And without faith, many won't find the strength to stand for what's right when it costs them.

So, let's move from knowing how things work to exploring why we live and lead the way we do.

Faith and Morality

Politics can give us laws, but it can't give us character. It can set boundaries, but it can't make us good. That's why, before we talk about reviving our country, we must talk about reviving the heart both individually and nationally.

In this section, I'm going to be honest about my own failings, clear about my Christian faith, and unapologetic in my belief that without God, our revival will be short-lived. You don't have to share my faith to read on but I hope you'll at least consider why it matters, and why it has shaped so many decisions I've made, both in politics and in life.

Because if we're serious about restoring this country, we must start here. Before we talk about economics, education, or immigration, we must look at who we are as individuals and who we are as a nation. That means confronting not only our systems and structures, but our souls.

I'm not perfect, and I don't pretend to be. But I've come to believe that the moral confusion and cultural decline we're living through is not just a political failure, it's a spiritual one. And no politician, law, or policy can fix what only forgiveness, truth, and grace can.

This section begins with the foundation of Christianity and ends with one of the hardest topics of all: abortion. In between, I've tried to show how faith isn't just about Sunday mornings or personal belief. It shapes how we forgive, what we tolerate, how we treat our bodies, and how we value life itself.

These chapters aren't about guilt-tripping anyone. They're about revival. And if we want to revive our country, we have to revive our conscience first.

Christianity

After politics, some might find it odd that the next chapter is about Christianity. But for me, it's not odd at all. It's the foundation beneath everything. My decisions, my values, my hope for Britain, my hope for a revival; all flow from my faith in Christ.

Sadly, the West too often wants to silence anyone who speaks openly about their Christian faith. Can you imagine having a gift so precious, so amazing, so real and yet feeling unable to share it? That's how many believers feel today. I made a promise to myself: that I would take every opportunity to speak up. Not to become an annoyance, but to be faithful. So that when I meet my Maker, I can say: I tried. And this chapter is another attempt to spread the Good News.

It therefore follows that out of all the chapters in this book; this is in my opinion probably the most important. In fact, it's the one that links them all together. If we simply followed the Ten Commandments given to Moses on Mount Sinai (generally things not to do) and then followed the teachings in the Sermon on the Mount given by Jesus (generally things to do), then this world, this home of ours, would be a far better place.

Let me begin with the most famous verse from the bestselling book in the world. John 3:16: "For God so loved the world, that he gave his only Son, that whoever believes in him should not perish but have eternal life."

That verse tells us something extraordinary: heaven is yours, if you simply believe in Christ and repent. How wonderful is that? Literally, all you have to do is believe in Him and you are saved. Repentance which is admitting and turning away from our sins, is required, and this is a commitment, not just a one-off gesture. But if we do that, His promise and His grace are secured.

It doesn't matter who you are, what you've done, or how far you've drifted. The offer still stands. That's the power of the cross. That's the beauty of the Gospel.

Following Christ won't always be easy. It will mean turning your back on old habits, walking a different path, and standing firm when others don't understand. But it will also be the best decision you ever make. Let me briefly explain the *Bible* and the Gospel and what we mean when we talk about the Trinity.

The *Bible* is made up of 66 books, 39 in the Old Testament and 27 in the New Testament. The first five books of the Old Testament explain how God created the world, how humanity fell into wickedness, and how God saved Noah and his family through the great flood. He gave us the rainbow as a promise never to flood the earth again.

The *Bible* then tells the story of Moses and the Ten Commandments, and the laws God gave to His chosen people. We have books of poetry (such as the Psalms), books of wisdom (such as Proverbs), and books of prophecy, foretelling what was to come.

Then we reach the New Testament. This tells the life of Jesus Christ, through the Gospels of Matthew, Mark, Luke, and John. His virgin birth. His miracles. His teachings including the Sermon on the Mount. And, ultimately, His betrayal, His crucifixion, and His resurrection. Jesus died on the cross for our sins. And He rose again, conquering death, to offer us eternal life.

We read in the Book of Acts about Christ's ascension to heaven. The coming of the Holy Spirit, our helper, sent by God. And the early church.

The following letters (or "epistles") give practical guidance on how to live out this new faith, and how the early churches succeeded and struggled. The final book, Revelation, is a prophetic vision of what is still to come.

So, when we speak of the Trinity, we mean: God the Father (the Creator), God the Son (Jesus Christ, our Saviour), and God the Holy Spirit (our helper and guide). Three in One. Distinct, yet united. This is the God I follow. Not distant. Not vengeful. But loving, forgiving, patient and powerful beyond measure.

Most of us will have heard of the Ten Commandments, but not everyone the Sermon on the Mount. As this entire book is about explaining a variety of subjects to those who may have never heard or thought of them before, I couldn't speak of the *Bible* and Christianity without listing these here.

Given by God to Moses on Mount Sinai, the Ten Commandments are not suggestions. They are commands. They form the foundation of biblical morality, and millennia later, our own laws still reflect them: 1) You shall have no other gods before Me. 2) You shall not make for yourself a carved image. 3) You shall not take the name of the Lord your God in vain. 4) Remember the Sabbath day, to keep it holy. 5) Honour your father and your mother. 6) You shall not murder. 7) You shall not commit adultery. 8) You shall not steal. 9) You shall not bear false witness. 10) You shall not covet.

If we're honest with ourselves, we've all broken some of these. And if we're even more honest, our lives would have been better had we not. I hear many say, "I don't need God to be good." But often, we compare ourselves only to the worst lawbreakers, murderers, thieves, rapists. Yet if these ten laws were so important that God inscribed them onto stone tablets, perhaps we ought to take them seriously. Perhaps it's time for humility, and maybe even forgiveness.

Then there's the Sermon on the Mount. These are called the Beatitudes. In this sermon, Jesus took the law to a heart level: Blessed are the poor in spirit. Blessed are those who mourn. Blessed are the meek. Blessed are those who hunger and thirst for righteousness. Blessed are the merciful. Blessed are the pure in heart. Blessed are the peacemakers. Blessed are those persecuted for righteousness' sake.

Jesus didn't replace the Ten Commandments; He fulfilled and strengthened them. In the Sermon on the Mount, He raised the bar from action to intention. "You shall not murder" becomes "turn the other cheek." "You shall not commit adultery" becomes "cut out the lustful eye." "You shall not lie" becomes "let your yes be yes and your no, no."

I once heard Mel Gibson say that "you can't help the first look but you can control the second." That stuck with me. The same applies to our thoughts. We may feel jealousy or anger but we don't have to let them fester. We can train ourselves to become better people. Even for non-Christians, there's wisdom in this. What good does envy do? What good does unforgiveness bring? None.

Jesus finishes by saying, "Everyone then who hears these words of mine and puts them into practice, will be like a wise man who built his house on the rock." If we all build our lives on rock, trust me we will have a much better life.

I can't talk about Christianity without sharing my own story. I was brought up in a Christian household and, like many in the 1970s, went to Sunday School. But as I entered working life, I lost interest. Then, in my late thirties, after getting married and having two children, I decided to take them to church. That's when I gave my life to Jesus.

It didn't happen immediately. I didn't think I was good enough. I thought, "I'll try to be a better person first, and then I'll make that decision." Now, I wasn't a criminal. I was probably like 99% of people. But still I thought I wasn't good enough. Eventually, I realised the truth: I was never going to be good enough. The truth is none of us are. And that's okay. One day, I simply asked Him to come into my life. And He did. I repented of my sins and made a promise to follow Him. I've never looked back.

I know I'm a better person. My wife has a better husband, and my kids ended up with a better dad. My life hasn't been a bed of roses since then, but it's been so much better. I've been able to speak in places I never imagined, knowing Christ is by my side.

The confidence and comfort He gives me in every situation is something to be cherished. I genuinely believe it's made me a better businessman and a better friend. Of course, I fail but I fail less. And when I do, I'm forgiven by my Maker and, when I try to make things right, often forgiven by those I've wronged too.

So why include Christianity in this book? Because every chapter connects back to it. Men and boys? Treat them with kindness, and they'll treat women and girls the same. Forgiveness? Needed more than ever. Politics? Should be about helping our neighbour, not ourselves. Pride? We don't need to celebrate tolerance we should live it. Minimum wage? Treat others as you would want to be treated. Parents and children? Honour and love must go both ways. Every issue in this book would be improved through Christian values. I challenge you: find a chapter that wouldn't benefit from giving reverence to our Lord.

Many ask: Why believe in a fictional God on a fluffy cloud? I get it. It's hard to have faith in something you can't see. But there are plenty of invisible things we believe in the air we breathe, the wind, gravity. We see their effects, and that's enough. People call it blind faith. But we've been given a book, the *Bible* (the world's bestselling book) to guide us.

Here's a question no one's been able to answer for me: Where does life come from? Darwin's theory explains how creatures may evolve and adapt but it doesn't explain the spark of life. Life only ever comes from life. A seed looks dead, but when you plant it and water it, life returns. The seed came from a living flower. Something or Someone had to give it life and us life. I believe that Someone is God.

Jesus Christ was a real historical figure. First-century texts confirm His existence. His disciples died awful deaths to proclaim that He rose from the dead. Would they have endured that for a lie? It's not my job to convince you, however. It's my job to tell you, the rest is up to you.

Christ is waiting for you. No matter what you've done, if you're ready to repent and believe, He is ready to forgive and not only give you eternal life, but a better life right here.

I think, deep down, we all know there's something more. But in the West, it's become easier to believe in nothing, so we can live as we please, without accountability. The irony? We want others to treat us well to follow the Ten Commandments. We want politicians to speak plainly, to be honest, to serve others. We want a better world, yet we reject the one faith that could help us live better lives. Quite bizarre, isn't it?

There are so many misconceptions about being a Christian. One of the biggest is that it's just another religion a set of strict rules and limitations. But it's the opposite. Christianity isn't primarily about religion or rules; it's about a relationship with God. Yes, we've spoken about the commandments, but these aren't there to restrict us. They're there to guide us, to help us build our lives on a solid foundation. God only ever wants the best for us.

I know many people haven't had the benefit of a loving father, so it's hard to relate. But if you can imagine the best dad in the world and then multiply that by infinity, you might get somewhere close to the love God has for us.

Another common misconception is that Christianity is a crutch for weak people. There's no denying that I lean on Christ, but I can tell you I've been far braver, far more resilient, and far more determined with God than I ever was without Him. So no, it's not a crutch it's more like a turbo boost. It strengthens the areas where I was weak and sharpens the areas where I was already strong.

As for the idea that it limits your life. Again, totally wrong. Only through a relationship with our Heavenly Father do I believe we truly appreciate the world we live in, the people we share it with, and the abundance He's willing to pour out on us if only we ask.

I remember the film Limitless, where a man takes a pill and suddenly has incredible intelligence and clarity. That was Hollywood. But I tell you truthfully: I've had mornings, after real time with God in prayer, where I've woken up and felt I could take on the world. That I could be an MP. That I could be the best dad. That I could write a book. That I could grow a business, be a better husband, make real change. And the more I spend time with Christ, the more I try to live how He wants me to live, the more I seem able to do.

You're reading the proof. Who would've thought a 'sparky' from Armthorpe would one day write a book, after being an MP, marrying a truly wonderful lady, and raising two great kids? And I'm not done. God has more for me, and He has more for you, too.

This book was written for many reasons. To help me try and make sense of the madness we're all seeing. To help others understand why it's so hard to change things. But it was also written so I could include this chapter to speak of the wonder of faith in God.

If you've read this far and you feel something stirring inside you that quiet nudge, that warmth, that thought you can't shake, don't ignore it.

That's the Holy Spirit. Our helper, sent by God. He's inviting you to take the step I once took. Don't wait. I waited and I regret doing so.

There is a great life and an eternal life waiting for you. Go grab it.

Forgiveness

"Not forgiving is like drinking rat poison and expecting the rats to die."
— Anne Lamott

Not the nicest way to open a chapter but perhaps one of the most important subjects this book will touch upon.

We've all been wronged, or at least felt wronged, at some point in our lives. Friendships have ended. Business partnerships have collapsed. Customers have been lost. Worst of all, families have been torn apart. I've seen it firsthand: mothers and daughters not speaking, fathers and sons estranged, brothers falling out. Bonds that should be unbreakable broken. Sometimes over the silliest of things. Sometimes because someone meddled. And sometimes, because of a deep breach of trust.

The tragedy is, it's rarely just the two people involved who suffer. Whole families are affected. A grandmother unable to see her grandchild. A little boy missing his grandad. The ripples of unforgiveness spread far and wide.

If we're ever to move forward, individually or as a society we must understand this: unforgiveness holds us back. It doesn't just wound us. It damages us.

I grew up in Doncaster, a town shaped by coal mining. Places such as Armthorpe and pits like Markham Main were the heart of our community. Men worked side by side, risking their lives and forging bonds that lasted a lifetime above ground and below. They trusted each other like brothers, their friendships solidified by danger, hard work, and shared sacrifice. It wasn't quite like the frontline, but not far off and it happened every day, not just in times of war.

Then came the miners' strike of 1984. And everything changed. Some men stood firm and stayed out. Others, facing financial ruin, returned to work. They were labelled "scabs" a word still whispered with bitterness today. What once united these men began to divide them. Lifelong friendships were lost. Streets fell silent. Communities fractured.

Forty years on, the anger still burns. Some are still furious with those who went back to work. Others blame the unions. Others still, the police or the Conservative government. Resentment has lasted lifetimes. People have died carrying it. I understand it was a dark, difficult time.

But the inability to forgive didn't just damage relationships, it damaged entire communities. It damaged the North. And it opened the door to political complacency.

In places like Doncaster, bitterness toward the Conservatives became so entrenched that Labour politicians took these areas for granted. They treated them as safe seats, doing little but expecting loyalty. All because of unforgiveness. It wasn't a lack of money that left us deprived, it was a lack of good leadership. And a community paralysed by the past.

Unforgiveness doesn't just live in politics or industry. It lives in our nation's history.

The Troubles saw horrendous acts of violence carried out. The Good Friday Agreement of 1998 brought peace, at least on paper. The bombs stopped. The army withdrew. Power-sharing began. It was a remarkable political achievement. But real forgiveness doesn't come from politicians. It comes from people on the ground. And that's the harder question: have the people forgiven?

Many, I suspect, have. Many just want to get on with their lives without fear. Kids are wonderful at bringing broken communities together. They just want to play, and it takes a truly scorned individual to stop a child from kicking a ball in the street. Some people chose not to hate, but to love.

But there are also many who lost brothers, fathers, or children and simply cannot forgive. Sadly, that bitterness may well pass down the line. And who are we, if we weren't part of that history, to judge?

All I will say is this: those who do find a way to forgive are the ones who show real strength. Real courage. Forgiving after decades of hate where families have lost real loved ones and still being able to move forward…that's true forgiveness. Often done quietly. Often not even spoken about. Just happening. The kind that occurs not at negotiating tables, but over cups of tea in broken homes.

Wow. Just wow.

Sadly, for many, the scars remain. Murals still divide Belfast. Walls literal and emotional still separate communities. Catholic and Protestant children still grow up apart. Often taught two versions of the same history. There's peace, yes but not always reconciliation.

Forgiveness doesn't always mean forgetting the past. It means choosing not to be ruled by it. And that applies in Northern Ireland as much as anywhere else in Britain.

I must also clarify that forgiveness does not mean justice shouldn't be served. If we've been wronged and there is criminality involved, justice must be done. But we can still forgive. Forgiveness can often look like weakness, especially when someone appears to be "let off." So no, justice must be done. But forgiveness must follow.

I've never been wronged like the people I've just spoken of. I have however been wronged in business. I've been wronged by friends and acquaintances. I've worked in Parliament and that can be a difficult place. But I've chosen not to bear a grudge. Yes, I guard my heart, but I have forgiven. And I hope the people I've wronged have forgiven me.

Families can sometimes be the most hurtful places and often the place where it's easiest to make a mistake. Some of the most painful divisions I've witnessed have been in families. Couples separating. Children used as pawns in a game of resentment.

Yes, people let each other down, we're human. We all make mistakes. Some of them big. But if we could learn to forgive even if we don't reconcile the damage could be reduced. Children could still see both parents. Mum could still rely on Dad. Families could share the same room without tension. And over time, with enough healing, some families might even find their way back together. But it only starts with forgiveness.

What about those who've already passed? I've met people who carry grudges against the dead. They let loved ones go to the grave without ever forgiving or being forgiven. Why?

Sometimes we hold on to resentment because it gives us someone to blame. "I didn't succeed because he held me back." "I drank because she said that." "I couldn't cope because they did this."

Forgiveness usually takes two. But when one of them is gone, is it still possible? Yes. In fact, sometimes it's easier. All it takes is letting go and trusting that if they had another chance, they'd want peace too.

I'll talk more about personal responsibility later in this book. But when we finally take ownership of our lives, when we stop blaming others, when we forgive, maybe even forget, and move forward, everything changes. For us. For our families. For our communities. And yes, for our country.

I can already hear the alarm bells in some people's minds: "Should we forgive everything?" My answer is yes but as I've said, forgiving doesn't always mean forgetting. And it certainly doesn't mean repeating mistakes.

You might forgive an abusive partner but that doesn't mean you move back in with them. You might forgive someone who broke your heart, but you don't offer it blindly again. Forgiveness is strength. But so is self-protection. Guard your heart. Forgive, yes but learn. And protect yourself. Because when we do, we all win.

We also must learn to forgive ourselves. That can be the hardest part. Some of our greatest wrongs came through selfishness, carelessness, or lack of thought. Others were deliberate. Some were things we couldn't help.

But Christianity is powerful when it comes to forgiveness. It says we must forgive and that includes ourselves. But first, we must repent. Turn away from what we did. Decide not to do it again.

Sometimes, that opportunity has passed. The deed is done. The moment is lost. The person we wronged may have moved away or even died. Maybe they were a child who just wanted our time, and now they've grown up. That time can't be reclaimed. Which is why forgiving ourselves is often the hardest step. But it must be done.

We are not meant to live miserable, guilt-ridden lives. That helps no one. We must forgive. Repent where we can. Apologise where we can. And if we can make up for the time lost or the trust broken we should.

I can't talk about forgiveness without speaking as a Christian. I've made plenty of mistakes. You don't get to 53 without racking up quite a few. Thankfully, most of the people I've wronged have forgiven me. There's one relationship I still need to mend, and I will before this book is done. But the greatest forgiveness I've ever received is from my Heavenly Father.

The *Bible* is the greatest story of forgiveness ever told. God gave His Son to forgive our sins. Whether or not you're a Christian, you know the story. You've seen the cross.

God forgives me for everything. And if He can do that, surely, I can forgive others. And so can you.

Swearing

I really do not like swearing. It's called foul language and that's exactly what it is: foul. The very word means dirty and smelling bad. Not good, is it?

Yet, it's everywhere now. And worse, it's increasing. Across all walks of life. Once, it was the language of the working man, often heard on the shop floor, down the pits, or in the fields. But that's usually where it stayed. It trickled into the working men's clubs but rarely when women were present.

Most could switch it off and on. You didn't swear in front of your mum or you got "a clout round the ear." In the armed forces, it was apparently common, but even then, I doubt it was used toward senior officers. It was just part of everyday language among soldiers, usually in high-octane situations.

Women, though, were historically criticised for using bad language. The phrase "fishwife" was a derogatory term because fishwives were known to curse. When men swore, it was rough; when women did it, it was unladylike. Why? Because ladies didn't swear. Or at least, they weren't supposed to.

But the rules have changed. Now, you hear it everywhere. TV is full of it. It used to be censored but not anymore. BBC dramas are laced with it. Women swear as freely as men now. If that's equality, I'm not sure it's progress.

What's worse is how it's crept into the mouths of children. Now, I'm not naïve, kids have always experimented with swearing. It was often a way of feeling grown up. But even then, it was done out of earshot of adults. And if an adult did hear, you were in serious trouble.

Not anymore. Now I hear it out of the mouths of babes.

When a six-year-old tells their mum to "f*** off," you know it's over. That child's future is already compromised. Why? Because it signals a lack of discipline and respect. And a child who grows up without those is a child heading toward trouble, possibly prison.

And yet, this is fixable. But only if our leaders, influencers, writers, and content creators grasp the impact of their own words. Those who use social media to spread profanity, who script it into every line of a drama, who think a message isn't powerful unless it's laced with expletives, they're part of the problem.

I spent the best part of five years in Parliament. Many down there bear titles such as "Honourable," "Right Honourable," "Lord," "Baroness," or "Sir." And yet so many of their mouths are foul. They want to lead but set examples not fit for the farmyard and then wonder why society is disintegrating.

I've heard the argument: "It's just a word. What's the big deal?" But I've also been told many times that "words matter" especially when I've said something a minority group didn't like. So, if words matter in one context, they matter in all. And foul language matters.

So, what's the answer? Don't use it. Simple. Train yourself not to swear, ever. People often get caught out using it when they shouldn't, but if you never use it, you never get caught out. Just like muscle memory and yes, I did Taekwondo, your vocabulary becomes what you practise. If you only practise clean speech, clean speech becomes your default.

As for film and television? Some say you can't be realistic without swearing. Maybe that's true in some stories. But I'm not so sure. Many of the most critically acclaimed films ever made are nearly all free of bad language or use it only sparingly.

Take Casablanca, Vertigo, Jaws, Schindler's List, Remains of the Day, Dunkirk, The Boy in the Striped Pyjamas, The Constant Gardener. These are stunning films deeply moving and culturally significant, without being foul-mouthed. And one of my favourites, Tom Cruise, manages to make dozens of box office hits without leaning on swearing.

People say dramas based on true stories need to include swearing. But if the story and the acting are powerful and they so often are, the message will land without it.

No matter how you look at it, there really is no need for foul language. And if we take responsibility and trace the path backwards, from the mouths of our leaders, through our screens, down to the children in our streets I think we all know, deep down, that we could and should do better.

One final thought. People often say it's too late, that the cat's out of the bag and there are bigger things to worry about. But I believe a revival starts with the small things. The things we can control. The words we choose. The example we set. Because if we don't, the real danger isn't where we are, it's where we're heading.

The next chapter is on free speech. And at first glance, that might seem ironic. But as you'll see, free speech comes with responsibility. And how we speak links directly to what we're allowed or even forced to say. That's not ironic at all. That's exactly the point.

Free Speech

"I disapprove of what you say, but I will defend to the death your right to say it."

— Evelyn Beatrice Hall (writing as S. G. Tallentyre), 1906

What is free speech? The ability to say what you want, wherever you want. Is it important? We shall see.

Free speech is the cornerstone of any healthy, functioning democracy. Without it, we are simply soulless bodies fed with what the state wants us to consume. We should be able to express our thoughts, challenge ideas, question authority, and poke fun at all, without fear of punishment. That used to be the norm in Britain. Now, it feels like it's becoming a risk. Let us look at some examples.

The boats. I'll cover this in more detail in another chapter, but for now, ask yourself: what if no one had called it out? What if no one had challenged what was happening? What if no one had pointed out how angry the British public were feeling? You might think the government isn't trying hard enough to stop the problem and I'd agree. But believe me, they know exactly how we feel. Why? Because people spoke up. They used their voices. They exercised their free speech.

What if no one had questioned the madness of the trans ideology? We are in no way in a good place with this yet. But without challenge, so many more innocent lives would have been damaged. That's free speech at work.

Let us look at a more practical example. What if no one had said anything when people were dying because they weren't wearing seatbelts? Or about the dangers of drink-driving? Debate changes things. Sometimes for better, sometimes for worse, but without it, there's only silence and submission.

The problem with free speech, however, is that people say things we don't want to hear. The problem without it is that people stop saying anything at all. This is a tough chapter to write.

Of course, there's the other extreme saying anything and everything, regardless of the consequences. But is that enough reason to ban free speech altogether? I don't think so.

There was a time in this country when you couldn't say anything negative about the monarch. Free speech was suppressed under the rule of kings and queens, and speaking against the Crown could get you branded a traitor.

Parliamentary privilege, introduced with the Bill of Rights in 1689, gave MPs the ability to speak freely in the House of Commons. It meant we could raise uncomfortable issues without being dragged into court for it.

The 19th and 20th centuries saw further liberalisation, though blasphemy and obscenity laws stuck around for years. In 1998, the Human Rights Act incorporated Article 10 of the European Convention on Human Rights into UK law. This granted freedom of expression but with limits. Speech considered hateful or dangerous to national security can still be restricted. So yes, free speech in the UK is protected, but it is not absolute. And in recent years, many believe it's being quietly suppressed again.

The USA is often seen as the gold standard. Free speech is protected by the First Amendment of their Constitution: "Congress shall make no law… abridging the freedom of speech, or of the press…" Even hate speech and flag burning are protected. But here's the key: the First Amendment applies only to the government. Private companies like social media platforms can still delete posts or ban users. So yes, you can say almost anything in the U.S., but that doesn't mean social media companies have to host it.

France takes free speech seriously, with protections dating back to 1789 in the Declaration of the Rights of Man and Citizen. It declares: "The free communication of ideas and opinions is one of the most precious rights of man." But like the UK, France has limits. Hate speech, Holocaust denial, and certain types of religious defamation are banned. After the Charlie Hebdo attack in 2015, global debates erupted over how far free expression should go.

China's constitution technically guarantees freedom of speech. But that's only on paper. The Chinese Communist Party controls everything, the internet, media, education, even private chat groups. The "Great Firewall" blocks Google, Facebook, YouTube, and foreign news sites. Surveillance is everywhere. People can be jailed for simply sharing a meme criticising the government. So, while China claims to value free speech, its reality is complete state control.

We are not anywhere near China yet. However, things in the UK are definitely moving in the wrong direction.

We only have to look at what happened during the summer of 2024. Some people were prosecuted and in certain cases jailed for social media posts. While some posts were vile, many felt the punishments were harsh. The result? People stopped speaking. They feared the consequences. That is censorship, plain and simple.

I believe in full free speech. But it comes with responsibility. Think of it like owning a Mogwai from Gremlins harmless at first, but dangerous if misused.

In the film, a father buys a cute Mogwai and is given strict instructions: don't get it wet, don't feed it after midnight. At first, it seems sweet and safe. But once the rules are broken, it multiplies into gremlins that tear a town apart at Christmas.

Free speech is the same. Used properly, it's a blessing. Abused, it can quickly turn destructive.

If someone incites violence, and someone else commits murder, where does the blame lie? With the murderer, obviously. But what about the person who fuelled that hatred? What if the victim is someone you love your partner, your child? You might start thinking differently about consequences. Again, I say, this is tough. Let's imagine a world where we can only speak what the state allows.

Take the Thalidomide tragedy. This drug, given to pregnant women, caused severe birth defects. The manufacturers denied it. Some doctors ignored it. It was investigative journalists, particularly *The Sunday Times*, who broke the story.

Despite legal threats, the paper pressed on. They exposed the scandal, forced compensation for victims, and changed drug testing laws forever.

Without freedom of the press, without freedom of speech, that injustice might have been buried.

Some say, "Fine, let journalists speak, but not individuals." But that's wrong. Individuals often spot the problem first. The press usually follows later.

Sadly, there is a cost for speaking up. Tommy Robinson is a good example of what happens when the media stays silent and an individual takes the heat. He broke a court order by posting a video. Was that illegal? Yes. But many argue free speech should have protected him. I don't believe he incited violence, but what if someone had acted on it? That is always the risk. So where do we draw the line?

Parliamentary privilege allowed me to speak freely, and I used it. I once stood in the House and spoke about immigration. I told a story: a British family with a young daughter. Next door lived another family with a young girl. The two girls played together and the families were friends. Due to work the neighbour moved and a landlord bought the property. Four men moved in. They didn't speak English. They didn't care for the property. They shouted outside late at night.

I also described an A&E department where few seemed to speak English. I called out the liberal elites who preach kindness but never live with the consequences. I knew what I said would spark outrage. I was branded a racist. Compared to Enoch Powell. The media went wild. But hundreds, thousands of people told me they finally felt heard. That's what a MP is supposed to do.

Social media has changed the game. We're all broadcasters now. A single post can reach millions. That was unthinkable 30 years ago. But people treat it like a private chat. They post in anger, or after a drink, and regret it. Once it's out there, it's out there.

I've learned, sometimes the hard way. You know whether something is controversial within ten minutes of posting it. That doesn't mean it was wrong. But it might upset someone. And yes, I care about that. I don't post to offend. But I know I can offend. That comes with the territory. My advice? Sleep on it. Don't post when angry. Don't post drunk. Free speech is your right but the consequences are yours, too.

Some free speech hits harder than others. Take Ricky Gervais. He's someone who upsets me, not because of what he says about me personally, but because of how he speaks about Christianity. I know he thinks he's being clever. I know he's trying to be funny. But I also know the damage it can do.

One of the most powerful things about Christianity is the comfort it brings to people who are isolated, grieving, or struggling. Someone ill in hospital. Someone trying to feed their family. Someone being bullied at school. A Christian believes that God is with them. That He can help. That He will help, in His time. That belief might be the only hope some people have.

When someone like Ricky mocks that especially on a huge platform, it chips away at that hope. Not everyone has a strong enough faith to just brush it off. Ricky has wealth, fame, and fans who hang off his every word. People think, "He must know what he's talking about." And so, they believe what he says. Trust me, he doesn't. He has no explanation for how this wonderful world came into being.

People may say I criticise illegal immigrants and ideologies such as trans and I do. But I also offer solutions. I feel a duty to protect the people I was elected to represent. I don't call for surgery or suppression; I call for counselling, care, and truth. Ricky doesn't offer anything in return. In my view, his routines take hope away and replace it with nothing.

He can surround himself with applause, success, material things but when you rob a vulnerable person of their only hope, you take everything. That's why his words bother me. I don't like them. I think they do harm. But would I ban him from saying it? No.

What I can do is choose not to listen. So, I don't watch him now. I don't follow him now. And I'd encourage you to do the same. That brings us neatly to cancel culture, especially in our universities.

This is one of the worst modern trends. Like I said, I don't like Ricky's material, so I wouldn't pay to see him. But would I cancel his shows? Never. If people want to hear what he has to say, they should be free to do so.

Venues and organisations that cancel bookings because someone might be controversial should be ashamed of themselves. They've broken a pact with their audiences, with free thought, with society itself. If people don't want to attend, fine. If they want to protest peacefully, fair enough. But cancelling someone altogether? That's weak. That's wrong. And for this to happen in universities, it's terrible.

Universities should be the one place where every view is heard. They should be where ideas clash, where students are encouraged to think critically, challenge assumptions, and sharpen their own beliefs. Instead, we see vice-chancellors pandering to "outraged" students, and speakers disinvited because they expressed something unpopular. That's not strength. That's not education. It's a failure of leadership.

I said in Parliament once that we should be creating warriors, people who can listen to something they disagree with and respond with courage and conviction. Not cancellation. Another recent example of cancel culture, one I cover more fully in later chapter is abortion.

Individuals have been arrested or charged even for silent prayer outside abortion clinics. Let that sink in. Meanwhile, other chants at protests, including religious slogans, are often tolerated without challenge. And yet this is supposed to be a Christian country. So, what's happening here?

The reason is simple. Some individuals who originally protested outside abortion clinics didn't know when to stop. They went too far, showing graphic images, confronting vulnerable women, and turning what may already have been a traumatic moment into something worse.

Now, I don't agree with abortion. Not at all. But I can also acknowledge that it must be, in most cases, a horrific and painful decision for any woman. I doubt many do it lightly. Therefore, is it fair for her to be aggressively challenged in the street? I don't think so. And as I have said before, it's not always what you say, it's how you say it.

Do I agree with banning prayer zones? No. It's a dangerous precedent. But again, free speech comes with responsibility and when we don't exercise that responsibility with tact and respect, we hand the state an excuse to interfere.

And what about those chanting "Allahu Akbar" at pro-Palestine protests? Should they be allowed? If we truly believe in free speech, then maybe they should. But then why the double standard?

Is it that the government is more sympathetic to one cause than another? Or is it simply that when the numbers are so large, they don't want to upset the crowd? I think it might be a bit of both.

So how do we keep free speech alive, without the state getting involved? By thinking. Call out injustice, of course but do it respectfully. Don't incite violence. Challenge those who speak hatefully. But also challenge those who call out injustice without respect.

If we do this, we keep free speech alive while keeping society stable. It might sound idealistic. Maybe it is. But it's better than the alternative, being told what to think, what to say, and when to shut up.

Because here's the truth: we either put up with what we don't want to hear, or we put up with being told what we can hear. And I know which one I'd rather live with.

Just one final thought: if people can't say what they want because others are scared it might incite violence, won't that suppression cause violence anyway? I told you this was a tough one, didn't I?

Porn

Porn is probably one of the most difficult subjects to talk about.

If it ever gets mentioned, it's usually ignored, the subject changed, or it's laughed off. Someone else is watching it, never us. And women? Of course, they never watch it either. Really? No. Sadly, that isn't true.

The statistics are quite astounding. 70-80% of men and 30-50% of women in Western nations reportedly view porn regularly.

Now, I'm not convinced those figures are entirely accurate. They're quoted often enough, so there's probably some truth in them. But if hardly anyone admits to it, where are the numbers coming from? Presumably from downloads, views, and site traffic. Still, whether you trust the data or not, one thing is for certain: porn is definitely being watched. And if you dig a little deeper, you'll quickly begin to understand why so many are concerned. Let's have a little history first.

Pornographic imagery goes back to ancient times. Greek and Roman pottery and frescoes often featured explicit scenes. The Kama Sutra, written in India around 400 AD, contains graphic illustrations. Early erotic art was often tied to fertility rituals or religious practices.

With the invention of the printing press, erotic books such as The School of Venus (1655) were distributed, usually underground. Governments tried to clamp down on it: in the UK, the Obscene Publications Act of 1857 aimed to outlaw such material. In 1953, Playboy was launched, and soft-core porn entered the mainstream. In 1972, hardcore pornographic films began hitting cinemas, ushering in what many called the "Golden Age" of porn. By the 1980s and '90s, VHS tapes brought it into people's homes, still limited by access and cost.

Then came the internet. Some even argue that porn is what made the internet take off so quickly. After that came smartphones, the iPhone, and then websites like Pornhub. It's now so readily available that one click can show you the most explicit acts imaginable.

So how bad is it, for the viewer and for the people actually taking part? If you search online for "dangers of porn," you'll find endless studies, reports, and warnings. Dr Valerie Voon, a neuroscientist at the University of Cambridge, studied the brains of regular porn viewers and found patterns similar to those seen in drug addicts.

Watching porn literally distorts how the brain functions. Many families have broken down due to one partner's obsessive use of it. It is addictive, and just like a drug addict needing a stronger hit, viewers often seek out more extreme and explicit content over time.

And it's not just about addiction. The feminist movement, quite rightly in many ways, has long criticised porn for how it diminishes and objectifies women. It encourages sexist attitudes and reinforces the idea that women are simply there for male pleasure.

That said, the reverse is also true. On a recent BBC drama, a man was ridiculed for being impotent due to drinking too much. It seems the BBC thinks it's fine to mock men and treat them like objects too. It's not. However, you look at it, there's always someone damaged by porn.

There's also a darker criminal side to all this. Parts of the porn industry have been linked to organised crime, trafficking, and exploitation. The demand for ever more extreme content fuels abuse. Watching it isn't harmless, it helps sustain that system.

The demand for more and more extreme content has fuelled an industry that profits from misery. By watching it, you're not just a passive observer, you're taking part in something harmful, possibly criminal, and certainly degrading, either to yourself or to someone else.

Many people might be surprised to learn just how many women also watch porn. But apparently, a lot do. And they are just as affected. The same brain chemistry applies, dopamine spikes, desensitisation, addiction. The consequences hit both sexes.

For women, the damage is often different, but arguably even more severe: lower self-esteem, body dissatisfaction, confusion between societal "sex positivity" and personal discomfort, even sexual dysfunction. If their partner is watching porn, many women feel body-shamed or inadequate. But this goes both ways now. Men, too, are now being compared and judged.

We're now seeing a rise in porn-induced erectile dysfunction, especially in men under 30. Long-term use is increasingly linked to isolation, emotional detachment, relationship breakdowns, increased aggression, and completely unrealistic expectations.

To me, there is no such thing as "ok" porn. Just like bad language in films (see my chapter on swearing), it adds nothing of value. If ever there were a clear example of a slippery slope, this is it.

We've gone from the cheeky innuendo of family TV to the light titillation of 'Carry On' films to soft porn like Confessions of a Window Cleaner and then fast-forwarded to full-blown hardcore porn available 24/7. And now we have so-called "stars" boasting online of sleeping with hundreds, even claiming 1,000 men in a single day.

How sad must your life be if you're that young woman? And how sad is it that 1,000 men wanted to take part in that? What on earth does that say to our young people?

I know some won't like me saying this, but whether they're 18 or 40, I honestly don't know what kind of parent raises someone to think that's acceptable. It's heartbreaking that both performer and participant treat it as normal.

I've tried to write about topics people are afraid to address, and I always like to offer some kind of solution. In this case, I'm not sure I can.

AI might make things worse in one sense, by creating ever more realistic synthetic content. But maybe, just maybe, it will remove the need for real people to be involved. Will it get rid of real-life porn stars? No. But it may reduce the scale of what we're seeing. Still, the deeper problem remains: if people want to see it, they'll find it.

So, what can be done? Start by delaying phones for children as long as possible. Social media companies must take some responsibility. But as a parent, you can't just switch the Wi-Fi off they have 5G. You can't rely on filters, they're cleverer than you. So instead, delay the smartphone. Give them an Alexa or a normal alarm clock. Set rules. Stick to them.

And when they're old enough, set the example. Put your own phone on airplane mode at 10 p.m. No devices in the bedroom. If you've seen porn and feel ashamed, don't stay stuck in guilt. Forgive yourself. But stop watching it. It truly will ruin your life and for what? You are worth more than this.

And to the adults reading this, deep down, you already know it's not right. You don't need me to tell you. If you laugh about and share images, stop. It is not helping. Porn is an addiction, but you can stop. Smoking is extremely addictive, often a 20-a-day habit, yet people still manage to quit. So, if smokers can stop, so can you.

Think about the lives that have been wrecked to put this in front of you. Think of the chain of criminality you are supporting by taking part. Is that what you really want to be part of? Would you want one of your loved ones to be part of this industry? Your daughter, your niece, your son? I'm sure not. No one likes a hypocrite.

If we want to revive our country, we must start by reviving our minds. Pornography may seem like a private matter, but its impact is public and permanent. It weakens character, damages relationships, and cheapens what it means to be human.

You can't build a strong society on weak foundations. And if we can't control our desires, how can we lead, protect, or raise the next generation?

We need backbone. We need faith. We need a better example. And it starts with each of us saying: enough.

Abortion

I am pretty sure no girl dreams of one day having an abortion. I am sure many dream of having a baby. I am sure most women don't take this decision lightly. I am sure most women love their babies.

This subject is one of the most controversial in this book, especially written by me, a man.

But whether we like it or not, the laws around abortion are made by men and women across the political spectrum by politicians. And I don't think we can or should have a democracy where men only make decisions about subjects that affect men, and women only about those that affect women. So, I'm afraid, for those who don't want me to write on this, read or don't read, but write I shall.

Let's get to the facts. In this country, it is legal to terminate a pregnancy up to 24 weeks or up to birth on grounds of fetal abnormality. This is the highest limit in Europe. It came about because 24 weeks was considered the point at which a baby could survive outside the womb, though babies have survived from as little as 21 weeks.

We were also one of the first European countries to adopt such a policy, setting a precedent ourselves rather than following others. That still begs the question: as so many countries have a much lower gestation period for legal abortion. Why have MPs voted to remove any legal deterrent against self-induced abortions all the way to birth.

Yes, several attempts are being made to stop it from being criminal to terminate a pregnancy at full term. It looks as though they are going to be successful too. The argument is that no woman should ever be criminalised for an abortion. But with "pills by post" still available, and no need to see a doctor in person, this only increases the chances. At 38 weeks a baby is fully viable. Allowing self-induced abortions that late should remain criminal.

There are seven legal grounds for abortion under the Abortion Act 1967, but most fall under the catch-all that continuing the pregnancy would pose a greater risk to the physical or mental health of the woman than ending it. This has created an almost abortion-on-demand culture. No proof is required. As a result, 98% of abortions fall into this category.

Since the Abortion Act, over 10 million babies have been aborted in the UK. The numbers have remained fairly consistent, with a gradual rise over time and a sharp peak during Covid.

So, my searching question is: why so many? Research gives many answers. Too young. Still in education. Not emotionally prepared. Financial hardship, especially for single women. Unstable relationships. Coercion. An absent father. Feeling overwhelmed. Mental or physical health fears, even if not diagnosed. Pregnancy disrupting work, studies, or life plans. Failed contraception. Or simply a change of heart.

I can, and I'm sure you can, understand all these situations. But I'm not sure how much genuine support is offered. Were women ever asked: What support would have helped you keep the child? Did anyone encourage you to continue the pregnancy? Was adoption considered, and if not, why not?

In a liberal society, we will inevitably have liberal doctors. Some sign off sick notes with barely a question; others are more cautious. Surely abortion consultations are subject to the same inconsistency.

The activist crowd, the "my body, my choice" brigade, has played a huge role in the legalisation and normalisation of abortion. But are they ever there to pick up the pieces? Many women suffer greatly with remorse and regret for aborting a baby, especially for reasons unrelated to health or quality of life.

While writing this, I searched for stories that might help you think about this journey a little bit more than what the establishment seems to want us to.

First is Catherine Adair's story, a former Planned Parenthood employee (USA): "I had an abortion in my early 20s. At the time, it felt like the only way out of a crisis. But it didn't solve anything, it created a lifelong wound. I cried for days, but no one told me that would happen." She later left her job at Planned Parenthood and became a pro-life advocate, saying she saw firsthand how women were rushed through the process with little counselling.

Second, we can read Rachel's story from Rachel's Vineyard UK. This ministry runs post-abortion healing retreats. One anonymous account reads: "I was told it was just a clump of cells. But I held my stomach the day after and whispered, 'I'm so sorry.' The pain didn't go away. It just got buried."

My final story is from an anonymous British woman in her 30s, BBC, 2021: "I had the abortion at 18. I thought I was being sensible. But not a day goes by that I don't think about how old my child would be now. I never told anyone until I was 30. It eats away at you."

Common themes in regretful accounts are rushed decisions or feeling pressured, lack of informed consent or awareness of alternatives, grief lasting decades, especially around birthdays or due dates. Many didn't speak about it for years and a desire to warn others, silenced. Voices are often shouted down, especially if you're a man trying to speak up for life.

Which brings me to dads. It takes two to make a baby, and while many men disappear, others want to be involved. Yet the law says men have no rights when it comes to stopping an abortion. If the child is born, the man is expected to pay but has no say in whether that child lives. You may agree or disagree. But these are the facts.

As I continued my research, a simple Google search reveals some shocking phrasing. One UK abortion website says: "Since you will pass the pregnancy at home, you can decide how you wish to dispose of the pregnancy remains. They can be flushed down the lavatory or wrapped in tissue, placed in a small plastic bag, and put in the dustbin." Put in the dustbin? This is a life.

As I said: I do not judge. But to speak like this and not feel some sorrow says a lot about where we are as a society.

As we saw with the Assisted Suicide Bill, language matters. That bill was renamed the "The Terminally Ill Adults (End of Life) Bill". Easier to digest than the reality. The same is true here: "passing the pregnancy" or "pregnancy tissue" is easier to accept than calling it what it is: a baby. A human life.

The British Pregnancy Advisory Services (BPAS) or should it be called the British Termination Advisory Service, which carries out 43% of all

UK abortions, mentions psychological impacts but simply states they are "variable." No further detail. It even says, "You may see signs of life," then moves on.

BPAS has a turnover of £56 million and a surplus of £5.6 million. They oversee over 100,000 abortions a year. If this were any other business, we'd be asking: Are financial motives shaping their work? Fair questions.

Especially when you learn BPAS and MSI fund other pro-choice campaigns and charities. If taxpayers fund this, then why not fund pro-life groups with the same amount instead?

I know some will say restricting abortion harms women. But if it's harm we're trying to reduce, shouldn't we also consider the women who've lived with pain and regret for decades?

I cover buffer zones in my chapter on Free Speech. Buffer zones now prevent people from offering alternatives or support to women near clinics.

There were shocking reports: baby toys with fake blood, people spitting, filming women, graphic placards, hymns blasted through megaphones. That's not right. However, these were exceptionally rare in the UK.

Some protestors had gone too far. But maybe, just maybe, if more people were properly educated about abortion, we wouldn't have protests or buffer zones at all. As I wrote in my chapter on Free Speech, it's a sacred right. But it comes with responsibility.

I cannot speak of abortion without mentioning the medical risks and the silence around them. I'm not a fan of abortion being taught in schools, but when it is, it's usually about rights, not risks.

And yet: Women with one abortion have a 25–35% higher risk of preterm birth. With two or more, the risk rises to 50–70%. Surgical abortion can weaken the cervix, increasing miscarriage risk. There are higher risks of placenta previa and placental abruption.

Some studies show that multiple abortions can increase the risk of preterm birth, miscarriage, or other complications. Others dispute this. But shouldn't we at least be talking about it?

As I said at the beginning, I don't think any woman sets out in life hoping to have an abortion. Most find themselves there due to choices usually shared with a man.

Rape is the tragic exception. I can only imagine that pain.

But most abortions happen for reasons already known before the couple slept together. Yes, contraception can fail, but not as often as we're told. Many abortions could be avoided if people just thought ahead.

I don't condemn anyone who's had one. I don't agree with it. But as a Christian, who am I to judge? What I can do is share the truth and the stories of deep regret many women carry for years.

40% of abortions are by women over 30. So are their partners. At that age, we should be able to look at the bigger picture. Most say it's about careers or money. I understand. But ask any parent what the best part of life is; it won't be the pay slip or the job title. It'll be their kids. Their grandkids. I have said elsewhere gravestones don't say: "Sarah; excellent lawyer." They say: Beloved daughter. Wife. Mum.

You are precious. Yes, you.

My final thought is: Let's reduce the number of abortions. Let's support women who could cope. Let's be honest; this is a baby, not just cells. Let's listen to dads. Let's begin by lowering the legal limit to 12 weeks and reduce further when we are in a better place with education and support.

Let's think before we have that unprotected sex in a moment of passion. Let's fund charities that seek to offer support to women who have unplanned pregnancies. Let's not judge. Let's forgive and let's help women who feel remorse forgive themselves.

But let's also be troubled by ten million abortions and if we're not? We should ask ourselves, why not?

Life is precious. I believe it is God-given and only God should ever take it away.

Final Word – Faith & Morality

I've covered a lot in this section. I hope it hasn't come across as too preachy. I've tried to be honest about my own failings, while staying true to my Christian beliefs.

I began this section with Christianity, and I was tempted to end with it. But I chose to start with it, because if you as an individual and we, as a country, are ever to see a revival, I honestly can't think of a better place to start.

Start by making that commitment. Receive Christ's forgiveness. Then forgive others. Then yourself. And finally, lean on Christ to help you with the decisions you've made and the struggles you still face.

If you trust on Him, help He will.

I'll say it once more: becoming a Christian was the best decision I ever made.

The Economy

We often hear that money is the root of all evil. That's not quite true. The full verse says, "The love of money is the root of all evil." In other words, money itself isn't the problem. It's what we do with it. How we earn it, how we spend it, and how we treat others along the way.

A strong economy matters. Not just because it makes us wealthier, but because it gives people purpose. It allows businesses to grow, families to thrive, and communities to stand on their own two feet. But today, too many policies punish success, reward dependency, and treat wealth as something to be ashamed of.

We need to reset that thinking. We need to get back personal responsibility, honest work, living within our means, respecting effort, rewarding risk, and using common sense.

This section of the book tackles some of the biggest economic issues facing our country, from the unintended consequences of the minimum wage to the housing crisis, the vanishing use of cash, and the high-cost confusion of Net Zero.

I've not written a full chapter on tax. That's a book in itself but tax runs through all of it. As a conservative, I believe low taxes, both personal and business, are the best way to achieve growth. Tax should be fair, simple, and never so high that it punishes the very people who are trying to make a difference.

This isn't just about spreadsheets or statistics. It's about people. Builders, shopkeepers, landlords, apprentices, homeowners, workers, and employers. When the economy works for them, it works for the country.

A revival of good fiscal policies that reward work, control spending, and build prosperity is now needed more than ever.

Let's begin.

Minimum Wage

If we are going to have any revival in the economy, we need to stop bringing in policies that damage it. This section on the economy deals with four areas of real concern. We'll start with the minimum wage.

Talking about the problems with the minimum wage is, political suicide. However, unless we address it honestly, we'll keep watching the slow death of small businesses or, at the very least, the inability of small businesses to grow into big ones.

Let's start with a quick history lesson. The minimum wage in the UK was introduced in 1999 by Tony Blair's Labour government. At launch, it was set at £3.60 per hour for adults aged 22 and over, and £3.00 for those aged 18–21.

We also had something called the Living Wage, which aimed to reflect the actual cost of living, but that distinction has faded. Today, in 2025, the minimum wage for those 21 and over is £12.21 per hour, with lower tiers for younger workers and apprentices.

Many other Western countries have adopted similar policies. But what they all have in common is a political shift to the left: governments more interested in sounding good than doing good. So, what's the problem?

First, it's a socialist idea. And like most socialist ideas, they sound compassionate, but rarely works in practice. Politically, it's clever. As I've said elsewhere in this book, there are more employees than employers. If you want votes, promise a higher minimum wage and paint yourself as a champion of the working class.

But I hope by the time you've read this chapter and this book you'll see through the spin.

Why was the minimum wage introduced? Because it looked good. It didn't initially cost the Treasury a penny. In fact, it raised revenue. When wage thresholds stay fixed, but wages rise, even the poorest start paying income tax and National Insurance. Employers also pay extra NI on these higher wages. So, a Chancellor can look generous while quietly raking in more tax. Win-win? Not quite. The money must come from somewhere.

First, it often comes from company profits, if there are any. Many people forget the full title of a business's accounts: "Profit and Loss." That's right, many companies lose money. In fact, many business owners, especially small ones, are now the only people legally paid less than the minimum wage. The one who had the idea. The one who took the risk. The one who pays the bills, the suppliers, the staff. Often working 60-hour weeks and earning less than the people they employ. But socialist governments don't care about them, never have. And yet we all should.

These are the people who earn, not claim. Who employ, even if only one or two. Who keep shopfronts open and high streets alive. If only every MP had to run a business before they took office.

Second, it comes from the customer. Prices go up. Who can blame the business? So now the worker who received a £40 pay rise finds £10 lost to tax and the rest swallowed by higher prices on bread, milk, fuel, council tax, coffee, you name it. Have they really gained? I will return to this.

Third, businesses squeeze their suppliers. But those suppliers are also businesses, facing the same pressures. So, the pain just gets passed down the chain, making survival harder for everyone.

Fourth, some try to boost productivity. Get more out of their staff. But here's the problem: the government has removed an employer's ability to reward hard work. You're allowed to pay more but how, when the baseline is already so high?

If one employee stacks 100 boxes an hour and another only 50, you'd want to pay them differently. But minimum wage laws make that nearly impossible. So, what happens? The high performer gives up, realising there's no reward for effort. Productivity drops. The business suffers. Eventually, a machine does the work of both faster, cheaper, and without complaining. Goodbye jobs.

One irony that made me laugh: we've had a so-called Conservative government telling businesses what to pay staff, while unions told the government what to pay its own employees. What a farce.

Finally, the cost might come from cutting staff perks or scrimping on cleanliness and maintenance. This results in unhappy staff, unhappy customers, and ultimately another shopfront closing for good.

So, before the next Chancellor boasts about a 10% wage hike, and before you vote based on that promise, I hope you'll think again. Politicians love the short-term applause, but we must live with the long-term fallout.

Some might say: "If minimum wage kills jobs, why are businesses still crying out for workers?" Fair question.

The answer is simple: when every job pays about the same, people choose the easiest one. This is called wage compression, and it's affecting many sectors, especially public services. I also address this later in the book in the chapter on police, but the problem runs deeper than just law enforcement.

There was a time when a police officer or a teacher was paid significantly more than a semi-skilled worker. Not anymore. Thanks to relentless increases in the minimum wage, semi-skilled roles, such as stacking shelves or driving delivery vans, now pay nearly as much as jobs that once carried much more responsibility, training, and risk. People ask themselves: what's the point?

Why take abuse in a classroom or face danger on the streets when you can earn the same, or close to it, in a warm supermarket aisle with less hassle? Well, hopefully.

Add in the fact that many young people, pushed through university, think they're above certain jobs and are holding out for their dream role. While others have learned to manipulate the welfare system so well that work just isn't worth it. Meanwhile, many of the hardworking young, the grafters, have fled this country, sick of seeing their effort unrewarded.

The result? Fewer people willing to work, because policies make not working more rewarding than working.

There will be many from the charity sector and the unions who say the minimum wage has reduced exploitation and narrowed inequality. Well, it may have lifted wages, but we've had the minimum wage for some time, yet we still hear about the "cost of living crisis." Surely both can't be true.

There is a lazy assumption that anyone on low pay deserves to be. But that misses the point. The question isn't always whether someone "deserves" more, it's also who pays for it, and what happens to prices, jobs, and opportunities when the government forces it across the board.

Many think the minimum wage is great, until their boiler breaks down and the apprentice is charged at £25 an hour. Or the price at the supermarket goes up, not because of greed, but to pay the increased wages of the person on the till. That's why this book and this chapter, matters. Understanding the connection between the minimum wage and how it affects us as consumers is something that charities, unions, and politicians don't want us to know.

And this is not just anecdotal. *The Sun* newspaper reported that:

"Emerging reports in the UK point to growing financial distress among SMEs. As of mid-2025, around 49,000 businesses are classed as in critical distress, with bars, restaurants, and travel sectors especially impacted. Rising minimum wage and employer NI costs are frequently cited contributors."

Across the Atlantic, a recent National Bureau of Economic Research (NBER) study of California's $20-per-hour fast-food minimum wage (AB 1228), affecting chains with 60+ outlets; estimated employment declines of 2.3–3.9% in fast-food jobs, equivalent to around 18,000 lost positions from 2023 to 2024, compared to national trends.

It is no coincidence that adult care budgets have skyrocketed of late. Why? Because many of the jobs are paid at or near the minimum wage. People often complain about inheritance tax. But if the minimum wage continues to rise, there may be very little left to tax after huge care home costs. Many may think that's fair. But whether you agree or not, it's another effect that those championing this policy often ignore.

I do like to try and offer solutions to the many problems I discuss. And I'm realistic enough to know that scrapping the minimum wage altogether wouldn't get any politician elected nor would it be right to do something so controversial without telling the public upfront.

So how about this: what if we kept a minimum but introduced bands? Banded Minimum Wage: Fairer, smarter, more motivating.

A starter band for new workers. A higher band for those who show up, try hard, and take responsibility. Not based on who you know, or what school you went to, but how you work. Imagine how many young people we could inspire again.

I'd propose a lower rate rise at the next budget, say, 3% above the current minimum, as a base, and 7% or more for those who've earned their stripes. It wouldn't solve everything. But it would start to restore reward for effort, respect for work, and a ladder to climb.

So, there you are: a relatively simple solution to a very complex and sadly, damaging policy. Maybe I've just ended my political career by writing this. But the hard truth is this: the real minimum wage is £0.

And when the entrepreneurs have given up, the shops have closed, and all that's left are state-backed corporates and liberal elites patting each other on the back, maybe then we'll realise what we've lost. But by then, it might be too late.

Housing

The first home I purchased was for £29,000 back in 1994. I was self-employed even then but had only recently been made redundant from a job that paid £5.47 an hour as a qualified electrician. Today, I pay my electricians around £19 an hour. That same house would now cost around £150,000. It needed a lot of work and so would a house at that price today. But just do the maths. In the past few decades, wages have increased three to four times, while house prices have risen fivefold. So even in Doncaster, where prices have historically been lower, the ladder is getting harder to reach.

The example I've just given is much worse in the South. We're now seeing places where average incomes are higher, yes but house prices have increased elevenfold. Wages just can't keep up. Some coastal regions have seen similar growth, which has quite literally priced out the very people needed to serve those communities.

A second home in St Ives might sound like a dream. But if the hospitals and GP surgeries can't get staff, and there's no one to serve your coffee or clean the streets, then that dream starts to lose its shine. As a capitalist and a conservative, I believe we should strive and achieve. But we also must take some responsibility. When a problem exists, that we can help with, we should be willing to try and put others before ourselves.

So how bad is the crisis? Many councils now have waiting lists in the tens of thousands. Not-for-profit housing associations often have lists just as long. The private rented sector can't meet demand either. Partly because landlords are leaving the market under pressure from every direction.

With house prices continuing to outstrip wage growth, many young people have simply given up. They've resigned themselves to renting for life, with no real hope of owning a home.

I'll try to explain many of the reasons behind the crisis. But unlike some of the other problems this country faces, there is a silver bullet. It's called basic economics. One word: scarcity. When demand outstrips supply, prices rise. The silver bullet is therefore simple, build more homes.

The problem is, we're not doing it fast enough. And there are far too many reasons why not. Reasons why supply can't keep up and demand won't stop growing. Let's look at supply.

Developers must shoulder some of that responsibility here. Land banking is not helping. Holding land back to wait for values to rise is wrong. Apparently, there are 441,000 homes that could be developed but aren't largely due to this practice. If land isn't being built on because of planning issues, that's a problem for the public sector to fix and it should. But if it's being held back for profit, we need to hold those developers to account.

I'm not saying change the law. I'm not saying tax them. But I am saying: let the public know who's responsible. Name them. Call them out. Publish a public register of delayed developments. Let people see who is sitting on land that could house their children. We hear a lot about corporate responsibility. A firm builds a patio in an old folks' home or sponsors a charity walk. All very noble. But doing all this while sitting on land for 441,000 homes is not right. Personal responsibility is not just an individual issue; it's a company issue too.

This leads to planning; the dreaded word. When I became an MP, I was told three things: don't get drunk, don't get caught climbing out of someone else's bed, and don't get involved in planning. And if you can only manage to avoid one of those, make sure it's the last one. It sounds like a joke, but there is truth in it. If there's one sure way to lose votes, it's by being on the wrong side of a planning decision.

I remember an episode of Gavin and Stacey where Pam is on the phone complaining about her mobile signal while organising a protest against a phone mast being installed to improve that same signal. That's the paradox. We all understand the need for more homes. We want our young people to be able to afford one. But as soon as someone wants to build those homes in our village, we object.

I understand, I really do. But again, we must look at the bigger picture. One thing councils must ensure is that the promises made during planning are delivered. If a development is approved on the basis that there'll be a GP surgery, pharmacy, community centre and school places, then those things must be built. Sadly, this is too often not the case.

Poor planning departments must be dealt with. Some are so bad that I've heard local builders say they won't even build in their own towns anymore. Simply because of the poor decision-making and constant delays. That's how bad it's got.

Ironically, planning is one of the few council departments that can actually generate income. But with the rise of working from home, long-term sickness, low pay, and rising workloads, the good officers who remain are facing an impossible job or fail to understand the urgency. Why? Because they've never run a business and always get paid the same whether the decision takes a week or a year. The result? Slow decisions, a lack of communication, upset residents, and frustrated developers.

While I'm dealing with councils, I must also raise the issue of empty properties. Over 100,000 homes sit empty across the country. Many are in the private sector, and landlords are penalized sometimes quite severely, through double or even triple council tax rates. But what about the councils themselves? I'll point locally: there are properties in Doncaster that have been council-owned and left empty for years. Why? It's time we asked not just whether we're building enough homes, but also whether we're using the ones we already have.

One way to unlock more housing while easing community tension is to prioritise brownfield sites. Unused land within existing settlements that can be redeveloped without touching the greenbelt. That should always be our first stop. Protecting green spaces and boosting housing stock don't have to be opposites. And to be clear: protecting the greenbelt doesn't mean never building on it. It just means treating it as a last resort, not the first.

We're also seeing new building techniques emerge and we should make more of them. After World War Two, thousands of prefabricated houses were built in a very short time. We've learned from the downsides of some of those techniques, yes but we also seem to be ignoring the ones that worked.

Today, McDonald's outlets are built in factories, transported in pieces, and assembled on-site. If we can do this with restaurants, why aren't we doing it at scale with homes? Maybe it's a supply chain issue, but as an MP I hardly heard this sort of housing discussed. And if we're in a housing crisis maybe we should.

This is a subject I know from the ground up. Why? Because for the first ten years of my business, that's what I did. I spent my time on building sites, whether working on someone else's property or my own. I'm an electrician by trade, so although much of the structure was already up by the time I arrived for the first fix; running the cables and by the time we were second fixing, installing sockets, lights, and fuse boards, the house was almost complete. Still, you learn a lot. You see how it all comes together. You spend time with everyone: the developers, the one-man bands, the big companies. You get a real feel for how it works.

A lot has changed over the past 30 years. Processes have sped up. Materials have (sometimes) improved. Labour is harder to come by. But fundamentally, housebuilding hasn't changed all that much. You still need a decent piece of land, good footings, a skilled bricklayer, joiner, roofer, plasterer, spark (that's me), and a plumber. Get all that in place, and you can build a house.

Once you have permission, the building doesn't take all that long. They often seem to 'fly up' but it's all the work getting to that first spade in the ground that causes the problems. As I say, I've been in the industry. All the builder wants to do is build the homes. But it seems every obstacle is put in their way. Things need to change.

The previous paragraphs dealt with the supply issues. Now let's look at demand.

Immigration: I cover this more in a later chapter, but it's impossible to ignore its impact on housing. If you bring in a million people, and you don't have a many thousands of empty homes waiting for them, then yes, you're going to have a crisis. It's simple maths. And we have never had that stock sitting there. Meanwhile, building takes time, sometimes decades. So even if you're pro-immigration, the system must match demand. Otherwise, the market can't cope.

Family breakdown is another major issue. Divorce rates may be declining, but only because fewer people marry. People still cohabit, still have children, and then still split up. One home becomes two. Then those same individuals often start new relationships, and two households become one again but not before the original split added strain to the housing supply.

University expansion has caused more problems. This demand is rarely mentioned, but it matters. The push for "Education, Education, Education" has come at a cost. We've sent millions of young people off to university who come back with a mortgage-sized debt and a degree that doesn't land them the job they were promised.

Many would have been better off leaving school at 16 or 18 and taking up an apprenticeship while living at home. But when they accept college places across the country, they need accommodation, homes that could otherwise have gone to families. It isn't the students' fault, yet the consequences ripple out. After graduation, many continue renting rather than moving back home, and their debt burden makes saving for a deposit almost impossible.

Then we have the investment issue. The baby boomer generation has passed homes down to their children, creating accidental landlords. Nothing wrong with that, a home is still a home, even if rented. But over the last two decades, housing has become an investment vehicle for many. And with government policy making it harder to earn a fair return as a landlord, more of them have turned properties into HMOs. Houses of Multiple Occupation.

These offer strong returns but can blight communities. They change the character of a street. Multiple bins clutter the streets. Many individuals coming and going at all times of day and night. Unkempt front gardens as no single person takes responsibility. Which has caused resentment in some areas. In time, locals move out, often selling at a loss. The cycle continues.

Elsewhere, investor demand continues to push prices higher, pricing out young families altogether. I've even heard of institutional investors such as pension funds buying up land to build rental-only housing. Good for returns, yes. But as I've said before: corporate responsibility isn't just about building a patio at a care home. It's about doing the right thing. And driving up house prices by design? I beg to differ.

So, what are the solutions? Ask the banks, developers, and government ministers and they'll say: shared ownership and longer mortgages. But this doesn't fix anything, it just inflates prices. Developers want higher sale prices (why wouldn't they?), banks make more from longer loans, and politicians want to be seen to "do something." But real leadership means facing the problem honestly, not papering over the cracks.

Some blame young people for spending too much on Starbucks and takeaways. And maybe there's some truth to that. KFC just announced plans for another 700 branches in the UK, someone's buying it, and it's not me. Nail bars, tanning salons, tattoo studios they're booming. And I'm not naive. Not all of them are above board, but many are clearly busy. Maybe people think, "I'll never afford a house, so I may as well enjoy myself." If that really is the mindset, it's a tragedy in itself.

The silver bullet is to deal with scarcity but there are many ways to deliver it, as follows.

Cut immigration to near zero until supply catches up with demand. Continue building homes at pace, but not by compromising on quality or community. Prioritise brownfield development over greenbelt expansion wherever possible.

End shared ownership and extended mortgage schemes, they only inflate prices. Call out publicly the pension schemes that are buying up land and homes. We shouldn't stop them, but the public should know who they're investing with.

Reform university entry. Stop pushing young people into degrees that won't benefit them. Encourage apprenticeships, especially in construction and engineering. This will help their prospects of owning a home and prevent future delays caused by a shortage of tradespeople.

Reduce stamp duty; slowly and carefully to avoid market distortion. Abolish stamp duty for downsizers, encouraging older homeowners to free up family-sized homes. Ban HMOs but only once housing supply has improved enough to absorb the demand without leaving people on the streets. They're destroying communities. Once supply improves, convert HMOs back into single-family homes. And stop vilifying good landlords. Let them earn a fair return without resorting to HMOs, they're needed.

If you are a landlord, be the kind of landlord you'd want your son or daughter to have. Deal with problems promptly. Keep in touch with your tenants or use a reputable letting agent. Whether you're an accidental landlord or not, you are one and that comes with responsibility.

Being a tenant comes with responsibility too. It's not just about paying rent, it's about respecting the property, the neighbours, and the agreement you signed. Keep the garden tidy. Clean the windows. Take pride in where you live. How we do the little things says a lot about us.

Report problems early, pay on time, and treat the house like a home. A great record of paying rent helps when applying for a mortgage, lenders notice it. Too many good landlords have been driven out of the market by bad tenants who leave a trail of damage or debt behind them. That only shrinks the pool of available homes and pushes rents up for everyone else. A healthy housing market relies on trust and that goes both ways.

We should also encourage prudent financial habits in young people. Saving should be a priority from an early age. Bring back incentives like the Help to Buy ISA. They worked. They helped young people take a real step towards homeownership.

Property ownership brings responsibility and pride. And if we want any kind of revival in this country, we need the next generation to have a reason to get up in the morning to be able to look at the fruits of their hard work and not feel as though they are forgotten, left behind, and without hope.

This is a massive issue. I can't solve it in one chapter. But hopefully, I've helped you see the problem more clearly and pointed towards some real-world solutions. As this book continues to point out, many of the issues we face can be helped by our own actions. Whether that's the first-time buyer, the developer, or the Secretary of State for Housing. We can solve this problem. We just need to want to, badly enough.

Cash

Cash is king. I've heard that a few times in my life and it's true.

I grew up in the days of the £1 note. I remember saving seven of them for a holiday when I was a young lad. A pound a day for a trip to Filey. I earned a bit of pocket money cleaning cars and doing odd jobs. I was so pleased with myself £7! That meant cans of pop, waffles, and maybe a toy or some crayons from a shop called Wrays. I think it's still there.

When I turned 13, I took over a milk round not the early morning shift, but the Thursday and Friday evening round, collecting payments door-to-door. By then, the £1 coin had replaced the note. That might not sound like much, but when it's minus two outside and you're fumbling for your wallet every few doors, the difference between a note and a coin is massive. You either felt your fingers or you didn't.

That sort of job made you good with money. Giving change from a £20 note when the bill was £5.73 was brilliant for mental arithmetic. It taught you discipline, confidence, and how to look people in the eye.

Times have changed. Not only do we all carry calculators in our pockets now, but tills also work out the change. And most of us don't even use cash anymore we pay with cards, phones, even watches. And that, right there, is where the problem starts.

As I said, cash is king, but sadly and very worryingly that's no longer the case.

Let us take a little walk back in time. We've used coins since around 600 BC, but in Britain, cash in a formal sense began in the mid-17th century. Before that, people traded favours, goods, and services, but that system was inconsistent and often led to arguments. Coinage brought order. Ancient Greece, Rome, and China all had early coin systems. The Bank of England began issuing paper notes in 1694, marking the formal birth of central banking in this country.

The 19th and early 20th centuries brought the Gold Standard, where currencies were backed by a fixed amount of gold. It helped build trust in money but collapsed in stages during the World Wars and the Great Depression.

Today's money is fiat currency. It's not backed by anything physical, no gold, no silver, but we trust it because the government says it's worth something. It works because we all agree it does.

The note still says, "I promise to pay the bearer…" but no one's walking into the Bank of England demanding gold. We use money to buy and sell, to exchange the value we've created through work, trade, investment, or even support from the state.

Britain once led the world in trade. The pound was the global standard until after World War II, when the dollar took over. Britain was broke and the U.S. stepped into the role of global superpower.

To this day, most international trade from shipping and insurance to commodities and banking is settled in U.S. dollars. The SWIFT system (the global bank-to-bank payment network) and nearly all major banks operate in dollars. Even central banks hold them, making up about 60% of global foreign exchange reserves in 2024.

Could this change? In theory, yes. But it's unlikely anytime soon. China and India are growing fast, but trust matters just as much as wealth and the world still trusts the U.S. more than it trusts authoritarian regimes.

Meanwhile, our day-to-day lives have gone digital. Many people, especially the young find cash a burden. When my kids get money from grandparents at birthdays or Christmas, I often take the cash and transfer the amount into their accounts. It's easier. It's what they're used to. Maybe I shouldn't. Maybe I should make them use it.

Cash usage is in free fall. In 2012, 54% of all UK transactions were in cash. By 2024, that figure had dropped to just 12%. I've mentioned young people, but it's not just them. I'm over 50, and I can be just as guilty. The difference is: I know the risks, and I make myself use it. Because here's the real concern.

If we stop using cash altogether, we risk changing the entire structure of our banking system. We move away from high street banks and towards something called Central Bank Digital Currency or CBDC. That's when the Bank of England becomes the main provider of money and every transaction is monitored.

As an MP, I sat in meetings where this was being discussed. I raised concerns then, and I still hold them now. In a cashless society, every single transaction can be tracked. That might not sound too bad until you consider what that actually means.

What if you support a political movement the state doesn't like? What if your views are considered "problematic"? What if the government decides to restrict spending on certain goods or services, based on ideology, social scoring, or compliance? What if they track your fuel use to "protect the environment"? What if they block you from trading with a company because it hasn't signed up to a Diversity, Equality and Inclusion (DEI) programme? What if a director had spoken out on an immigration issue and the government froze contracts in retaliation?

We've already had glimpses of this. The Canadian truckers had their bank accounts frozen just for protesting. Nigel Farage has said he was debanked for holding views outside the approved narrative. What if you post something online, and instead of jail time, your access to your own money is revoked? This isn't science fiction. It's programmable money and it's already being tested.

Programmable money is digital currency with strings attached. Money that can be coded to work or not under certain conditions. And we're not talking about theories here. The Bank of England, the EU, and others have openly discussed these features.

Imagine a digital pound that only works in approved shops. Or expires if not spent within 30 days. Or can't be used to buy meat, or fuel, or alcohol. Or what if you say something "unacceptable" and suddenly, your money stops working?

In China, this is already a reality through their social credit system. In Europe, the digital euro is being explored, with proposals for built-in limits, sold to the public as "privacy features." In Nigeria, the eNaira failed not because of the technology, but because people didn't trust the control behind it.

All of this is being sold as innovation. Progress. Convenience. But it's really about control. Because programmable money turns your income into a leash. And someone else is holding it.

I once heard an analogy on the radio: Would you rather be given £100,000 that you could only spend on watching live wrestling or £20,000 to spend however you like?

Now, if you're a wrestling fanatic and all your friends and family are too, maybe the £100,000 sounds appealing. But for most people, it's obvious: the freedom to spend £20,000 on what you need is far more valuable.

And that's the danger of programmable money. You still get paid but you can only spend it on what the state allows. Only on approved products. Only at approved retailers. Only if you've met the criteria. It's not really your money anymore. It's credit with conditions. Scary, isn't it?

And it's not just about surveillance. A fully cashless society is fragile. It depends on power, internet, and bank networks. If there's a power cut, cash still works. If your card is declined, cash still works. If the broadband is down or a cyberattack hits cash still works.

Cash also helps small businesses. Card payments come with fees often 1.5% to 3% which eat into already tight margins. And when big payment processors go down, those businesses lose an entire day's trade. Cash gives them liquidity, control, and resilience.

So, when people say, "Only tax dodgers use cash," it's lazy stereotyping. Older people use cash. There are many vulnerable people who rely on it. The homeless can only use it. Kids learning money skills benefit from it. Supporting cash isn't anti-tech it's pro-choice.

Cash also changes how we think. Studies show people spend less when using cash. The friction of physically handing over notes makes us more careful. That's not bad it's sensible. It's budgeting in action. That little moment of hesitation when your hand reaches into your pocket. That's where wisdom lives.

Digital spending, on the other hand, feels abstract. Just a tap. Just a number. It removes that connection to value. And that plays right into the hands of marketers and credit companies.

Despite the decline in cash use, the amount of cash in circulation has risen. In 2014, around £60 billion was in circulation. By 2024, it was over £82 billion. Why? Because people are 'stashing' it. They don't trust the system. Sadly, many of us are sleepwalking into this.

Use less cash, and it becomes harder to use. ATMs disappear. Businesses stop accepting it. Cash limits kick in. AML (Anti-Money Laundering) rules make it difficult to spend large amounts. Try buying a holiday, a car, or jewellery with cash and you'll be met with suspicion or paperwork. Soon, it's just your groceries and a pint and even that's going.

You may ask what's the point in trying? Because if we use it, it's harder for it to be removed. Progressive governments will claim it's about tax avoidance. And yes, cash-in-hand trades to avoid VAT do happen. But let's be honest, big business dodges far more tax than you or I ever could. That's not an argument to punish ordinary people.

However, here's the dilemma; should we support places that only take cash? It makes me uneasy. Are they legitimate? Are they dodging tax? Are they funding something dodgy? I pay my taxes, why shouldn't they? It's a tricky one. We need to use cash, but we don't want to support the wrong people. That's the conundrum. The answer? Be selective. Use it with traders you trust.

This is a global issue. In the U.S., cash is still widely used. Mistrust of the state is stronger but even there, usage has dropped to 22%. In Sweden, it's as low as 5%. In India, a government move to scrap high-value banknotes overnight caused chaos hurting the poor most of all.

Even Sweden often held up as the cashless ideal has started rowing back. There's now a public debate about reintroducing cash protections for older and rural citizens.

Some people ask, "What about Bitcoin?" It's a fair question. Unlike CBDCs, Bitcoin is decentralised meaning no government controls it. That's partly why it appeals to those worried about surveillance or centralised control. But it's also volatile, poorly understood, and not widely accepted in everyday life. Am I saying it will never be a solution, no but its rise proves something important: people can sense that the system is changing and they're already looking for alternatives.

So, what can we do? As so often, personal responsibility is key. Force yourself to use cash, even once a week. Ask local shops to keep accepting it. Support those who do. Teach your children the value of coins. Make saving tangible. Let them see piles of pennies become something meaningful.

Ask your MP where they stand on CBDCs. If they haven't thought about it, ask why. If they support it without question, maybe it's time to elect someone else. Because if we don't act now, we'll wake up in a society where freedom is conditional, and access to your own money depends on your obedience.

Cash is king. Not the state.

Net Zero

If there's one subject that has caused huge upset and cost us dearly in recent years, it's the pursuit of Net Zero.

So, what is Net Zero? In simple terms, it means reducing our carbon emissions to the point where whatever we still emit is balanced by initiatives that remove carbon from the atmosphere. For example, if we burn a gallon of petrol that releases a certain amount of CO_2, we plant enough trees to absorb that amount. The net effect on the environment is zero.

That's a simplified explanation, but that's essentially it. And while carbon offsetting sounds good on paper, in reality it's full of holes. Trees take decades to grow, and we can't accurately measure how much CO_2 each one will absorb.

As for carbon credits, they're just a fancy way for big corporations to pay for someone else to go green while they carry on polluting. It's a box-ticking exercise that often balances the books more than the atmosphere.

I've even heard senior figures in medium-sized businesses claim that all their energy comes from green sources. Nonsense. Electricity comes from the national grid, which is powered in many ways. No individual or company can say with certainty that their electricity comes from one specific source.

What's really happening is that they're paying an extra penny or two per kilowatt to look good. Sad, but true. Their supplier may be investing in green energy, but until the entire grid is green, which could take decades, it's a practical impossibility to say your energy is 100% green.

The next question is: why reduce CO_2 emissions? CO_2 is a greenhouse gas. When sunlight hits the Earth's surface, it's supposed to reflect back into space. But CO_2 traps some of that heat in the atmosphere, creating a warming effect, like a greenhouse. Sunlight comes in, but the heat doesn't escape. That's why the ice caps are melting, and sea levels are said to be rising.

Now, this is a slow process. And because of that, many people remain sceptical. If you haven't been directly affected by extreme weather, it's easy to dismiss climate change. But does that mean every storm, flood, or wildfire is caused by it? No. Some are, no doubt. But many are due to poor land management: rivers not being dredged, overdevelopment, badly planned drainage systems. Fires in California, are they always down to heat, or are arson and poor forestry to blame?

Still, there are reasons to reduce fossil fuel use that are much more immediate. Anyone walking down a main road will be familiar with the dirty, choking fumes from diesel vehicles. Near airports and docks, the air quality can be dreadful. These aren't abstract theories, these are visible, breathable carcinogens. Trying to reduce that kind of pollution is obviously a good thing. The real question is: how should we do it? And that's where things fall apart.

The debate around how we reach Net Zero has become so polarised, it's tearing political parties apart. Some want to scrap Net Zero entirely. Who can forget, "Drill, baby, drill"? Others want to double down on it. What was once a matter of science and strategy has now become an ideology.

So, what's the truth? Is the planet warming? Yes, the data suggests it is. The ice caps are shrinking. But is this part of a natural cycle? The earth has been frozen before, are we just entering another "season"? Perhaps. The honest answer is I don't know.

But here's what I do know. We are burning fossil fuels. Fossil fuels release CO_2. CO_2 traps heat. So logically, the more we burn, the more we warm. That seems hard to argue with. The question the UK public wants to ask is: should Britain lead? Yes, the world should act. But should Britain take the lead? Let's look at what we've already done in the name of Net Zero.

We've shut down all our coal-fired power stations and closed nearly all our virgin steel-making plants. We tax cars so highly that people are scrapping perfectly good vehicles they can't afford to keep, while adding drugs to cow feed to stop them belching. We're covering productive farmland in solar panels. Shameful.

We're taxing every household via energy bills to pay for green initiatives. We import solar panels from China, where they're made using electricity generated by burning coal. You really cannot make this up, can you?

We pay, on average, four times more for fuel than many of our competitors. No wonder so many Small to Medium Enterprises (SMEs) are struggling. We still use more plastic bottles and convenience meals than most of Europe. We have huge gas reserves but choose to import instead. We plant trees everywhere to look green, then leave them to die. I have seen this with my own eyes.

You can see why people are fed up. And here's the kicker; the UK is responsible for just 0.9% of global CO_2 emissions. That's right, less than one percent.

China emits around a third. The United States comes second. We're 17th in the world. And if you look at emissions per capita, how much each individual emits, we're 64th. The average American emits more CO_2 than any other person on the planet. China, as a country, emits more overall, but per head, the average American does far more. We must ask why are we punishing ourselves while others carry on?

On the global stage, we've had leaders who bought into the dream of "leading the world" on climate change. COP26, hosted in Glasgow, was a prime example. Alok Sharma represented the UK and was desperate to get other nations on board, even pushing for the UK to fund climate schemes in developing countries.

That's right: not only are we taxing ourselves into the ground, losing jobs, and forcing industries abroad we're also paying other countries to go green. I like Alok, he's a good man but please surely everyone can see this is just too much.

Meanwhile, China hoovers up our manufacturing because it's cheaper to produce goods over there. And because their standards are different, the process can end up doing even more damage than if we made the goods ourselves. Then, of course, we ship the goods here, more fuel, more emissions, more hypocrisy. The irony is almost too much to bear.

I must admit I bought into it. At COP26, I really believed. I drive an electric car. I have solar panels. I even install them. That might sound hypocritical but I'm not against clean energy. I like my electric car (I have a petrol and a diesel one too). I'm not against reducing pollution or improving efficiency. What I'm against is crippling ourselves while the rest of the world does nothing.

I've often spoken about personal responsibility. When I was an MP, I heard so many children ask, "What is the government going to do?" like it was someone else's problem. "Why aren't they putting solar panels on our school?"

These were children, yes but it revealed something deeper. The throwaway lifestyle we've allowed them to adopt as parents, teachers, and government, has stripped away any real sense of personal responsibility. So many had plastic bottles of pop and water. So many had sandwiches wrapped in layers of packaging. So many were dropped off in 4x4s. So many will walk around in a T-shirt, no jumper, central heating set at 22 degrees while leaving the lights on when they leave a room (I do sound like my dad; he's a Yorkshire man too).

And it's not just kids with careless habits adults are guilty too. I recently quoted for a solar installation. The payback time? Twenty-seven years. I told the client. His reply? "It doesn't matter; it's a grant." And that's the problem. When it's someone else's money, nobody cares. But it's not magic money, it's our money. We should care.

If we are ever to truly tackle Net Zero, we must do it in a common-sense way, with the people, not against the people. And we must lead the next generation by example. If we don't, I fear the public pushback will be so strong that Net Zero will be scrapped altogether, wasting all the money already spent and achieving nothing. Or worse, if the pressure continues without consent, it could bankrupt the UK.

So, here's the ask and the solution. We should all take personal responsibility. Not because we're forced to, but because it's the right thing to do.

For me, it's plastic bottles. They annoy me. So, I don't buy them. I walk to the shop when I can. I make sure the kids switch the lights off. I do tell them to put a jumper on. [Smiles].

But if we all made small, sensible changes, without being taxed, punished and shamed into it and if the government supported innovation rather than enforcing ideology, then maybe, just maybe, Net Zero wouldn't be such a dirty phrase.

The government do need to 'back off' and take a good, honest look at what's really happening. Reset the targets. Get realistic. Scrap subsidies for technologies that don't work. Get rid of the green levies on our bills.

Champion new technology but don't subsidise it. Let capitalism do what it does best: give us all value for money. If we didn't tax our industries so much, we wouldn't have to subsidise them so much.

Embrace new technology. Nuclear reactors will have their place, I'm sure, but it doesn't sit right to make pensioners fund huge corporate projects.

Solar panels should go on rooftops, not farmland. So, let's put them there.

Let car and boiler manufacturers continue to invest in both existing and new technology. If we hadn't pushed for electric cars so hard, we may well have reached 200mpg in petrol or hybrid cars by now.

Heating our homes with hydrogen is still many years off. We'd all need to be connected to a hydrogen grid, and every boiler would have to be replaced. I've seen how hard it is just to get everyone on a street to contribute to adopting an "unadopted road" there's always someone who refuses. It will be the same with boilers. So, let's start replacing them with hybrid systems that can run on natural gas now and switch to hydrogen later.

Let's also continue the 'fabric first' campaign. Loft insulation, cavity walls, UPVC windows, all great. But spending tens of thousands of taxpayer money wrapping houses so tight they can't breathe, leading to mould? Not so clever.

Even if you don't buy into Net Zero at all, you must accept that one day we will run out of gas and oil, or it will become much harder to extract. If we can get that acceptance from the sceptics, and a bit of pragmatism from the eco-warriors, I'm sure we can all have our cake and eat it.

Because right now, those two words, Net Zero, spell nothing but upset, and a whole lot of cost.

Final word – The Economy

This is the last chapter in this section. I hope it's become clear that when government interferes too much, the wheels often fall off. Whether it's employment, housing, how we spend our own money, or as we've just explored our environment, overreach usually does more harm than good.

If this country is to have any chance of revival, we must remove the shackles from both business and people. That means lifting unnecessary taxes, cutting red tape, and trusting individuals to make their own financial choices. Do that, and businesses will thrive. People will take responsibility for their future. They might buy a home, start a business, or even employ others.

Either way, they'll have become stakeholders in this country, rather than just pawns. And when that happens, an economic revival won't just be possible, it will be inevitable.

But for prosperity to last, it must be nurtured in the right environment. And that environment is one of law and order. Without it, wealth cannot grow, communities cannot flourish, and freedom itself becomes fragile.

That is where we will go next.

Law and Order

Without law and order, nothing else works. You can't run a business if the tills are robbed. You can't raise a family if the streets aren't safe. And you can't build trust in your country if justice is inconsistent, delayed, or denied. That's as true for a thriving economy as it is for any other part of national life.

In this section, I look at four major areas where law and order are failing us: policing, prisons, drugs, and illegal immigration. These aren't just policy failures, they're moral ones. Because behind every theft, every assault, every overdose, every illegal crossing, there is a victim. Someone whose life has been shaken, whose trust in the system has been dented or destroyed altogether.

Our laws are supposed to protect the innocent, deter the criminal, and deliver justice for all. That only works if we enforce them. And it only lasts if the public believes in them.

As a Christian and a conservative, I believe in justice with compassion. That means proper policing, effective deterrents, fair punishment, and second chances where they are earned. It also means stopping the rot, saying what others won't, and restoring the authority our institutions have lost.

You'll find strong views in the pages ahead but also practical solutions from tagging over prison, to zero tolerance on drugs, to rebuilding police morale, to stopping the boats once and for all. This isn't about being harsh for the sake of it. It's about restoring order for everyone's benefit.

Because without law and order, there will be no revival and no hope of protecting the freedoms and fairness that should apply to every citizen, in every community.

Police

"The police are the people, and the people are the police."
— Robert Peel

I never actually saw a policeman clip someone round the ear, not in real life anyway. Is it true, or just a myth? One thing's for sure: as a young boy, I was always a bit wary of them. It was a respectful kind of fear. There was an open police station not far from my school, and I used to think, "I hope I never end up in there."

We saw bobbies on the beat too not all the time, but we saw them. You knew they were around. So, what's happened since? There seems to be little respect for the police these days. Most police stations are closed to the public, and you rarely see officers walking the streets. Let's try to answer why. And, as always, let's ask what can be done.

Most people have heard of Sir Robert Peel, who established the Metropolitan Police in 1829. That's why officers are still nicknamed "Bobbies." But what about before that?

In the 13th century, law enforcement was mostly down to local people. The phrase "hue and cry" comes from that time. If a crime was committed, the victim or someone nearby would raise the alarm, and villagers were expected to come out and help catch the suspect. It was chaotic and could be abused. If you had a grudge, it didn't take much to turn a mob against someone. And criminals if not caught could just move town, change their name, and escape justice.

Over time, things changed. Justices of the Peace were appointed. They relied on parish constables and watchmen, local volunteers, unpaid and untrained. Corruption crept in, as if they were paid, they were often paid directly by the victim.

Then came the "thief-takers" bounty hunters who caught criminals for a fee. Some became notorious, like Jonathan Wild, who was hanged in 1725 after it was discovered he ran a criminal empire himself.

The Bow Street Runners were the next step, formed in the mid-18th century. They were paid, trained, and did proper investigative work. They lasted until 1839, when the Police Act expanded Peel's Metropolitan Police model nationwide.

At first, people were suspicious. Uniformed officers on the streets looked like the start of a police state. Maybe they were right. Either way, crime and policing have changed massively since those days.

Crime has grown alongside the population. Mass immigration has brought in many people who contribute positively, but rapid changes have also created cultural tensions in some areas.

Then came the internet. A playground for fraud, grooming, cyberbullying, scams, blackmail, drug dealing, even terrorist recruitment. Add to that what many now call "policing of speech." Say the wrong thing online and you could get a knock on the door. You can see how the average bobby's workload has grown.

And to the latter point, many people are frustrated. Say the wrong thing online and you might have an officer at your door. But if your house is burgled or your car stolen, some say you'll be lucky to get a crime number.

Let's take a closer look with two examples. One: in 2024, police in England and Wales dealt with 1.35 million incidents of domestic abuse, that's one call every 23 seconds. Two: fraud. Nearly 18% of all reported crime is now fraud. These are serious offences, but they rarely make headlines. Unless it happens to you, you may not even know it's going on.

And that's part of the problem. We used to see the police on the streets, in our communities, even on TV. Shows like *The Sweeney*, *The Professionals*, *The Bill* gave us the impression that officers were tough, capable, and determined to get the job done.

Who could forget Jack Regan's famous line: "Get your trousers on, you're nicked." It gave the impression that crime was tackled head-on. Officers had discipline. They weren't afraid to act. Today, it's different.

We see plenty of crime on our phones but rarely see police in person. Stations are closed. Beat officers are rare. And criminals don't fear the consequences. But it's not just the criminals. Ordinary, law-abiding people feel the same. You call the police, no one comes, and you ask: "What's the point?" Unsolved burglary rates hover around 75% and it's even higher in some areas.

Worse still, the police themselves seem to have lost self-respect. I once saw a police car drive past a group of lads who were shouting abuse at them. The officers just looked ahead and kept driving.

When the public don't respect the police and the police don't respect themselves it can feel like society is unravelling? And yet we've more people behind bars than ever. So, it's not that no one's being locked up. But it hasn't stopped that growing feeling: that Britain is becoming lawless.

Something needs to change. Let's start with the principle: "The police are the people, and the people are the police."

That means we all have a role to play. We can't just leave it to someone else. We have to take responsibility for the little things. When someone behaves badly, call it out. When someone drops litter, challenge it. Respect for the police starts with respect for the rules and if we don't model that, who will?

We must speak well of the police in front of young people. Be honest, yes but don't tear them down in front of impressionable minds. If something isn't right, raise it through the proper channels.

The police themselves need to rediscover self-respect. If someone hurls abuse in the street deal with it. Challenge it. Ignoring it doesn't win hearts, it just signals weakness. And they must stop trying to be everyone's mate. Don't jump on every fashionable cause to look "inclusive" or "woke." Rainbow police cars? They're a laughingstock. People want effective policing not virtue signals.

Uniform should mean something. If officers don't look sharp, stand tall, and act with confidence, how can they expect the public to take them seriously?

We must end the DEI nonsense. Recruit on merit not skin colour, identity, or religion. And yes, recruit people who are physically fit, but also make sure they retain that fitness once they're through the door.

Officers spend far too long behind desks, drowning in paperwork. We need more of them out on the street.

On-the-spot fines work, so let's use them. And enforce them. AI can help with that. A fine that's not chased is a fine that might as well not exist.

Graffiti ruins an area. Most of us have driven into a foreign resort, seen the graffiti, and thought, "What kind of place is this?" It's the same here but we just accept it. We shouldn't.

If someone's caught spraying it, make them clean it. Put their face on Facebook. If they're under 18, put their parents' faces on too. Maybe then we'd take pride in where we live.

Rudy Giuliani introduced zero tolerance in New York in the 1990s. Squeegee men. Subway crime. He tackled it all. Police patrolled where crime was happening, not just where they'd always patrolled. The result? A city that felt safer. People cared. Criminals thought twice. It worked. We need that here.

What about the no-go zones? In some areas, including certain sites, police presence is minimal. Even when they know stolen property is there. How is that allowed? And protests? How can someone be arrested for silently praying, while thousands shut down a city centre week after week? It makes no sense. Either we haven't the laws, or we haven't the will. Either way, the police often look weak.

We might need something like the US National Guard. A properly resourced, well-equipped force that can respond to large-scale disorder or open defiance. If we can't create one, then give those powers to the police or the army. Standing by and doing nothing is no longer an option.

We also need to ask: who does what? Domestic abuse is serious, of course it is. But should police be the first responders to every case? Surely trained social workers could handle many of them. Police should still respond when lives are in danger, but heated family arguments aren't always a police matter.

Councils must know who the serious offenders are. And if they don't, they should. Information should be shared, and police should be freed up to deal with real crime.

Grooming gangs have exposed what happens when information is buried and cultural sensitivities are prioritised over truth. We've seen what happens when fear of being called racist stops justice. I have devoted a whole chapter to this. Why? it simply must never happen again.

County Lines gangs exploit gaps between forces. Our systems don't talk to each other. We have 48 police forces in the UK many using different software. That's madness. In a world of instant data, we've created a system that can't join the dots. We must fix it, fast.

And let's not forget rural crime. Quad bikes, diesel, tools, and farm equipment are stolen every week in areas where police presence is practically invisible. Farmers are often left to fend for themselves. That isn't good enough.

Online crime fraud, identity theft, scams are everywhere. But are police best equipped to deal with it? Most officers didn't join because they were brilliant with IT.

Maybe it's time for a truly dedicated cybercrime agency staffed by people who actually understand the tech. Use AI to help, and stop wasting police time knocking on 30 doors a day over a "naughty" tweet. I've had plenty said about me online; I just blocked and moved on. Teach people to do the same.

I ask a lot of the police force here and of the police officers themselves. So, we must discuss pay. Pay is a serious problem. Public sector wage compression is making it harder to attract talent. People look at less stressful jobs with similar pay and say, "Why bother?" Many officers stay just for the pension. That's no way to build a motivated force.

On top of that, many officers suffer mental strain, repeated exposure to trauma, and increasing physical assaults. We ask them to face the worst of society yet often give little in return. That must change.

Here's a thought: reduce pension, holiday, and sickness entitlements and give meaningful pay rises instead. Let people earn a decent wage now and take more control of retirement themselves later. It won't be popular with everyone. But it might work. It might help attract and keep good people. Because a demotivated workforce is bad in any industry but in policing, it's a disaster.

We all have a role in policing society. It starts with the little things, respecting the rules, calling out bad behaviour, and backing those that are paid to protect us.

The police must respect themselves again. They need to stop chasing popularity and start delivering results. We need officers on the streets, systems that talk to each other, and a real deterrent to crime.

Whether it's the police, the army, or a new National Guard, we need boots on the ground, powers that work, and officers paid properly. Because they take the big risks. They keep us safe. They deserve a wage and a public that respects them.

This isn't about blaming individual officers. It's about rebuilding a force that commands respect, not one that begs for it.

It can be done. It should be done. And we all must play our part.

> "The police are the people, and the people are the police."

Prisons

The thought of going to prison sends a chill down most people's spine. It's not just the idea of being locked up or having all your freedoms stripped away, it's also the horror stories of what happens behind those closed doors.

Films such as Escape from Alcatraz, The Shawshank Redemption, or more recently, Time with Sean Bean, don't exactly show prison in a good light. Time is probably the most realistic of them all but unless you've actually lived that life, none of us can really know what it's like.

I've visited and worked in these places. And they're not for me. But that's the point, isn't it? Are prisons meant to be a deterrent? Are they for punishing wrongdoers? For delivering justice for victims? To keep us safe? Or are they supposed to rehabilitate?

In truth, they should do all five. So, the questions we should be asking are: why are they so full? Do they actually work? And what can be changed to make them serve society better?

There are 122 prisons in England and Wales, 15 in Scotland, and 4 in Northern Ireland. In England and Wales, they're split into four categories:

Category A: high-security prisons for the most dangerous criminals.

Category B: closed prisons for those who don't require the highest security but still can't be trusted in lower categories.

Category C: training prisons, where prisoners are deemed unlikely to escape but still need some supervision.

Category D: open prisons though that term feels like an oxymoron.

There are 12 women's prisons in England. Scotland and Northern Ireland use slightly different categorisations but follow the same principles: the category reflects the sentence length, offence, and release risk.

We've been locking people up for millennia. In the 12th century, it was usually just a holding cell before individuals were executed. By the 15th century, many were imprisoned for unpaid debts, often indefinitely.

These were not places of justice or rehabilitation. They were filthy, corrupt, and more about profit than reform.

Things began to shift in the late 18th century. Penal reformers such as John Howard and Elizabeth Fry exposed the appalling conditions and pushed for change. Their work led to gender separation in prisons, better hygiene, ventilation, and even religious instruction.

The Victorian era brought in formal prison inspectors, moved prisons under state control, and focused heavily on discipline and moral reform.

The 20th and 21st centuries have seen waves of further reform, but the modern system is now plagued by overcrowding and understaffing. This, in turn, has led to riots and prisons becoming breeding grounds for further criminality.

If we look at what's happening today, we can see why there is overcrowding. We keep creating new laws and increasing sentence lengths. That is obviously going to cause overcrowding if we do not keep building new prisons.

So, they get so crowded, and then, just as quickly we're letting people out early. It's all political theatre. Tough talk with no substance. Sentences are given, but if there's no capacity or resources to back them up, what's the point?

What's the real difference between a 20-year sentence where the offender is out in eight, and an eight-year sentence served in full? Public perception. That's it. We pretend to be tough but rarely follow through.

So, what does prison life actually look like? I've visited four prisons, and while none of them were pleasant, they weren't quite the places the films suggest either. Being locked up from 5:30 p.m. to 7:30 a.m. is grim, but the days are usually filled with some combination of work, education, and exercise.

That said, there are long stretches of time when prisoners are just stuck in their cells. A lack of meaningful courses or a lack of motivation means this time is often wasted.

Visiting rights are limited. It's not the weekly family meetups people imagine, sometimes it's just twice a month. Prisoners can use phones on the landings, but they're costly and restricted. However, mobile phones are plentiful in some prisons.

Another issue is drugs particularly in private prisons. There are frequent reports of substances like Spice, cannabis, and other drugs circulating freely inside. But here's the problem: private prisons are run by companies, and every incident is a mark against their record. So, what happens? Incidents often go unreported.

In 2020, *The Guardian* revealed that HMP Parc, run by G4S, failed to log dozens of drug-related incidents because "it reflected badly on the contractor's performance." The fewer problems they log, the better they look on paper. But that doesn't mean the problem isn't there. In fact, it means it's more likely to escalate. That's dangerous, for staff, for inmates, and for the integrity of the justice system.

When someone is sent to prison, the consequences ripple outward. Often the main wage-earner is gone. Mortgages go unpaid. Families lose homes. Children are uprooted. The punishment doesn't just hit the prisoner; it hits everyone around them.

Let's not forget the victims. They're too often pushed to the sidelines in these discussions. Recently, some good has come from restorative justice programs, where offenders meet their victims face-to-face. It can help offenders understand the real impact of their crimes and feel genuine remorse.

But it helps victims too by allowing them to confront what happened, find closure, and sometimes even forgive. I don't always agree with prison as the answer. But we must always remember its five purposes: deterrent, punishment, rehabilitation, justice, and public safety.

With limited space and resources, we must use prison space wisely. So, who is inside?

One major issue is the growing number of people on remand, those who haven't yet been convicted or sentenced. Court backlogs are piling up, and this group grows by around 10% each year.

Building new prisons is slow, and crime rates aren't slowing down. The system is bursting at the seams, so what do politicians do? Release people early. Not because it's right but because they say, they have no choice.

Around 80% of the sentenced prison population falls into the following categories:

Violent offenders, drug offences, burglary and theft. Sexual offences, fraud, terrorism-related crimes. Immigration violations, domestic abuse and driving offences.

Whether you believe all of these deserve prison will likely depend on your own life experiences. If your home was burgled, you'll likely support a tough sentence. If someone assaulted your child, you'll want justice.

But what about someone who threw a punch in a pub after being provoked? What about a woman who snapped after years of abuse and hit her partner? Or a speeding driver who made a tragic mistake?

We all draw our own lines but if we remember those five principles deterrent, punishment, rehabilitation, justice, and public safety, we stand a better chance of getting it right.

One thing is clear: jailing people in 2024 over speech-related offences didn't help anyone. It didn't help the individuals, the prisons, or the public purse.

I've heard many stories of decent people who made one bad mistake and are now in prison costing the taxpayer £50,000 a year while a prolific burglar walks free.

So maybe it's time to step back and ask: what kind of country do we want to live in?

Could we ask victims what they want more often? Could we better track what works and what doesn't? Could we separate low-level financial crime or driving offences from serious, violent crime?

What about first-time offenders, should they be treated differently?

And what about those with long sentences? Surely there must be a meaningful incentive for good behaviour. Does releasing someone sentenced to 20 years after just 8 help anyone? No but releasing someone sentenced to 10 years after 8 gives hope and doesn't make a mockery of the law.

Is there another way? As Douglas Murray might say, tongue in cheek "there's always a Scandinavian example." Here are two:

Day Fines used in Finland, Sweden and Switzerland where offenders are fined according to their daily income. That means a millionaire pays more than someone on minimum wage. It's used for offences like driving, theft, and even minor assaults. It's fair. It's effective. And it avoids clogging up prisons.

Restorative Justice. Used in Norway, New Zealand, parts of the UK. Offenders meet their victims in a controlled setting. They talk about the harm done. They apologise. They agree on reparations sometimes financial, sometimes community based. It's not a soft option. But it's a smart one. And it works.

We've trialled versions of both in the UK, but we've not been bold enough to really commit.

We must also talk about prison staff. These people face constant abuse for little pay and even less recognition. As I mentioned in the chapter on the minimum wage, wage compression means you can earn more working in a warehouse than guarding a prison wing.

So, what's the answer? We need more prison space, at least to get back on an even keel. We need to clear the remand backlog and sentence people promptly.

We must look at each case individually. Consider the home life of the offender. Speak to the victim. Look at context. Intent. Circumstance. We need to stop passing laws that sound tough but do nothing in practice.

We need to expand the use of tags, name and shame offenders where appropriate, and stop pretending every crime is equal. We must make sure we always have space for violent, repeat, or predatory offenders so they always face the full weight of the law.

We must make sure that all prisoners have access to education, training and mentoring. I did, with limited success, carry out some mentoring at one of my local prisons. One prison is excellent at getting offenders back into work and never entering the penal system again. It does work if done properly.

Not every act of stupidity deserves a prison sentence. A young person driving a little too fast in a car doesn't belong in the same system as a career criminal. If they've killed someone, it's a tragedy but prison won't bring that person back. It might, however, turn that young person into something far worse.

Tags, fines, restorative justice, community work, yes. Locking people up at £50,000 a year only for them to come out more damaged than when they went in? No.

When we speak of honouring our public servants, that should include prison officers too. Pay them fairly. Train them properly. Support them always. Would I do that job? I'm not sure I would.

As you will have seen through this book, I am seen by many as uncompromising and tough on many issues. I understand fraud and financial crimes often ruin lives too, as does reckless driving, and they can't be let off with a slap on the wrist. But we must ask: do we want our prisons to work and keep us safe, or simply become a breeding ground for more criminality, more misery for both victim and offender, and a political theatre for bad decisions made by poor legislators?

I know what I would prefer.

Drugs

I hate drugs. Many people say not to use that word, that it's too strong but on this subject, I can't think of a better one. I genuinely hate drugs.

So many lives are wrecked because of them. So many criminals make money from the misery of others. And yet, it seems the government, the police, and even the public have come to accept that people take drugs. Yes, many talk tough "smash the gangs" and all that but in truth, they've given up. They're just going through the motions.

But can this battle ever be won? I live in hope.

Let's look at some of the statistics that show just how big the problem is. Around 9.2% of adults in England and Wales, about three million people reportedly used an illegal drug in the past year. Among 16–24-year-olds, that figure rises to 18.6%. Nearly one in five young people. That's not just worrying, it's a national disgrace. We should be ashamed.

So, why are so many young people taking drugs? Peer pressure, mostly. With so many using them, it's often seen as harmless, just a bit of fun. The people taking them often don't look like addicts. Their lives seem fine. It's just something they do on a Friday night. Add to that the way drugs are normalised or even glorified in films, music, and online, and it's no wonder.

I remember a line from Love Actually where Billy Mack says in a TV interview: "Don't buy drugs, kids. Become a rock star and people will give you them for free." Funny line, I laughed. But let's be honest: that sort of thing isn't helping. Cue the outrage "Nick Fletcher says a Richard Curtis film caused a generation of addicts." Don't worry, I've heard worse. But role models matter. A good one can stop a kid from ever touching drugs. A bad one can lead them straight into it.

But there's more to it. Many kids today are bored. Some are escaping abuse, school pressures, or broken homes. Many struggle with mental health. Others are simply chasing a thrill. Some follow celebrities, the same ones who joke about cocaine on talk shows or boast about their party habits. What's more dangerous than a joke is the growing push for decriminalisation. "Personal use" is the phrase they push. But that hides the real danger, especially for young people, who are often far more reckless than we ever remember ourselves being.

And let's not forget prisons which I covered previously. But I must mention it here too: there are many people who go into prison without a drug problem and come out with one. That can't be right.

Some kids are targeted by county lines dealers, as I explore in my chapter on Role Models. But as I write this, I realise that drugs touch on so many issues I cover in this book. That alone tells you how deep this crisis runs.

Some people argue, "I did a bit when I was younger, didn't do me any harm." Maybe not. But that doesn't make it right. And here's why: the so-called slippery slope is very real. I've heard it from countless former heroin and crack users. It starts by lowering your guard. You've done drugs once, so doing it again feels easier. Then you're chasing a bigger high. Then you're part of a culture: the dealers, the users, the networks. You're no longer dabbling, you're in.

Drugs vary in effect. Cannabis is seen as relaxing; cocaine, "Charlie," as a confidence booster. Many mix them with alcohol. Cocaine, like heroin, is highly addictive. What starts as a laugh becomes something darker. And then comes the tragedy.

I wish some of these so-called celebrities could be there when the police knock on a mum and dad's door. Watch their faces as they're told their child is dead. Hear the screams, the kind that cut through you. Screams of a life lost, and others ruined. I want that smug rock star or middle-class actor, the one who jokes about taking cocaine to witness that moment. Because whether they admit it or not, they've played a part.

And what life did that young person have before that dreadful day? A life of deceit. Of stealing. Of shame. Lived hour to hour, searching for the next fix. Sometimes you see them, begging on street corners. When you hand them money, you're often just feeding the habit. Some steal from their parents. Others rob tradesmen or shopkeepers. Either way, it's a miserable existence.

But here's what really gets me, the so-called casual users. The ones who just do a bit at the weekend. They are the biggest part of the problem.

Yes, the smart, sharp-suited professional with the nice car and lovely family. They are the reason this whole industry exists.

Most drug users in the UK are not addicts. They're recreational users. People who take cannabis, cocaine, MDMA, ketamine. They buy in small quantities. They pay premium prices. They rarely haggle. They fund the system. They normalise drug use. They make enforcement look ridiculous. And they help criminal gangs thrive. Because the same people who smuggle cannabis are often smuggling people. The same dealers selling MDMA are pushing heroin. The same criminal networks are involved in trafficking, child abuse, and violence. Every fifty-pound note spent on a line of coke props up that system.

Remove the weekend users out of the equation and the whole network could quite easily collapse. Demand drops. Prices crash. Dealers lose profits. And most importantly, fewer kids start using. So, if you're one of them, that bit of Coke at the weekend type, look in the mirror. Behind your lifestyle is a girl trafficked and raped, a tradesman robbed of his tools, a shopkeeper closing down. So, stop. And stop now.

Of course, many of these users are struggling and don't fully understand the networks they're supporting but they are still supporting them. They need to stop. And if they can't do it alone, they should have the sense to ask for help.

I can't mention drugs without speaking of County Lines. These networks as I will speak of in Role Models, target our kids. They mock the police. They use off-road bikes to cross fields, wear balaclavas on our Net Zero cycle paths, and act with impunity. These are serious operations run by fear. They prey on the young. They are the worst kind of criminal, and they are funded by too many people who think their fun is harmless.

The police? They go after the kingpins. But the moment one is jailed, another takes his place. The network stays. Just a new boss. I'm an electrical contractor. Remove me, and another director can step in. But remove my entire workforce, and I'm left with a pile of cable and sockets and no one to fit them. The business collapses. That's how we should fight this, break the networks, not just arrest one man. It's a lot of people to arrest, but I know tagging works.

Tagging helps an individual keep their job, stay at home, and if there's support rebuild. If not, it may mean rehousing. But even that's better than prison. It's more cost-effective too. Tags that detect alcohol already exist, and tech is moving fast. Tags that detect drug use will be a game-changer. I've met lads who wore tags. One told me that while the tag was on, the dealers stayed away. It gave him time to sort his life out. That's the kind of intervention that works.

So, what about other countries? Portugal and Sweden represent two extremes. Portugal decriminalised drug use. Sweden enforces zero tolerance. Portugal has reduced deaths. Sweden has reduced use. Britain? We seem to have both deaths and high use. Scotland's drug problem is the worst in Europe. Sweden has more crime linked to drugs, though that may also relate to its immigration problems. Portugal has open drug scenes and health issues, but less violence. And in the U.S. and Mexico, things are worse still. Their "county lines" is the Mexican border, where it's not just drugs, but people.

I believe zero tolerance is the only way forward. Blurring lines leads to a lack of respect and back to the slippery slope. What does zero tolerance look like? Literally that. We've sleepwalked into turning a blind eye to cannabis. We must enforce the law. Officers should arrest people smoking weed. Complaints of cannabis should be followed up. Sniffer dogs should patrol known hotspots. And yes, the legal process must be sped up but if it was, and offenders were tagged instead of jailed, we'd see a massive drop in this so-called harmless behaviour. That must be a good thing.

I've spoken at length about the why, who and how, of drug use. I opened with the misery it causes. But what about rehabilitation? Does it work? Is it costly? Is access easy?

Broadly, rehab can work but success depends heavily on the individual and the programme. If someone isn't truly willing, and if the programme is too short, then frankly, it's almost a waste of time.

The UK government's 2021 review by Dame Carol Black found that successful rehab requires more than treatment. It needs stable housing, employment support, and a strong recovery community. I heard of one house of multiple occupation where nearly every resident was an addict. One would try to go clean, but as soon as someone brought drugs back into the home, the rest would relapse. A revolving door of failure.

That's why the individual must be removed from their environment entirely. They need real time to break the addiction. And once clean, they need to be placed back into society with a job, a home, and a support network, all the things many of us take for granted.

But this isn't easy. It's expensive. Residential treatment can exceed £1,000 per week. And when 90 to 180 days are needed, it becomes a serious investment.

Is it worth it? I say yes. But it would be far better if the individual never started down this path in the first place. As with so many things prevention is better than cure.

So, here's my conclusion. Zero tolerance. Tagging, not prison for many. Stop normalising drug use. Shame the weekend users. Crush the cartels. Invest in real, long-term rehab. And yes, read my chapter on Role Models.

We may never win. But if we all take the same old principle of personal responsibility, we can reduce the damage. We might stop that knock at the door. We might prevent that scream of despair.

Because no parent deserves that. No police officer should have to do it. And no one should have to die for someone else's bit of weekend fun.

Boats

"Kindness without discernment leads to resentment."
— Many

"Stop the boats" is the rallying cry. But they keep coming. Why? In politics, as in life, a simple answer is always available; it's just difficult to do. It takes a backbone.

I'll give you the answer to this problem later. But first, let's look at some facts, figures, and reasons why previous, current, and future governments have failed, are failing, and will continue to fail.

Let's start by looking at when all this began. The small boat crossings began in noticeable numbers around 2018. Before this, migrants typically tried to reach the UK via ferries or the Channel Tunnel, often hiding in trucks.

The rise in small boat crossings coincided with increased security at ports and the tunnel, making land routes harder and organised criminal gangs switching tactics. We were also told the UK leaving the EU, complicated return arrangements.

I can hear the Remainers shouting, "Told you Brexit was a bad idea!" Sorry to disappoint, but the returns arrangement never helped. We did have, pre-Brexit, an agreement that allowed returns under the Dublin Agreement.

But here's the kicker: under the Dublin Agreement, more people were being transferred into the UK than were being sent out. By 2018, the imbalance had grown sharply. The system had become increasingly one-sided and ultimately ineffective for the UK. So, Brexit was a plus, not a negative.

The numbers are astounding. Since 2018 over 170,000 have made the crossing and the numbers are increasing year on year. There have been an estimated 152 deaths. Not that the smugglers care about that.

Now our current Prime Minister says he's going to "smash the gangs." I'm afraid that's simply not achievable. There are too many. And although we'll no doubt have some successes, as long as there's demand and it remains lucrative, someone will always be willing to risk it. Should we stop trying? Of course not. But will it stop the boats? Maybe a few, but not nearly enough to make a difference.

Sadly, like water down a mountainside, these people will find a way. And while our enforcement officers may care, they're ultimately doing it for a pay cheque. The ones coming across the Channel are doing it because they see a pot of gold, a new life, or perhaps reasons we don't yet fully understand. But the truth is this: the pull is stronger than our push. And therefore, they will always win. Our pushback needs to be stronger. End of.

I often hear; why do we ferry them in? The answer, it comes down to maritime law. Let me explain.

When the boat is still in French waters and not in distress, the French won't stop it. They are being paid by the UK government to prevent crossings, but once the migrants are in the water, the French just let them go. Why? Simple; they don't want them either. And if they were leaving our shores for France, would we stop them? Probably not. That doesn't make it right, but it helps explain why it happens.

You could argue that if France stopped them getting into the boats in the first place, they wouldn't go to France at all. It's a fair point but not one being made by anyone in power.

French authorities do track and observe many of the boats leaving their coast. But under maritime law, unless the boat is in distress, they don't intercept. The French government argues that stopping boats against the migrants' will; especially if they resist, breach international law, particularly the principle of non-refoulement, which prohibits forcing someone back into danger. Just for clarity, there are no international waters involved here. This is purely a UK–France issue.

One of my greatest frustrations is the RNLI. Like most people, I grew up admiring this organisation. I once watched as a young boy, a rescue at Flamborough Head. It was one of the most exciting sights of my childhood: the brave volunteers heading into rough seas, the boat shooting down the slipway, straight into the water. An hour later, they returned with four very wet men, embarrassed, but alive and well. The crew got a big cheer. Ready for the next call of duty. You never forget incidents of bravery such as that.

Sadly, that institution has now become a taxi service for illegal immigrants. Their mantra, like a surgeon's, is to protect life regardless of the circumstances and I understand that. But I also understand the public's frustration. We must remember however, the RNLI didn't put itself in this position. Weak politicians did. And it will take strong ones to get them out of it.

Whether it's the RNLI, Border Force, or our own Navy, the pattern is the same: the French let them go, and we pick them up. The thinking is simple: if we don't, they may drown. So at least protect life.

I've heard people say, "let them drown," but I don't believe they actually mean it. And even if they did, if they were physically there, I know they would step in to save a life. That's what makes us human. Is there an answer? We saw the last Conservative government try. So many different methods. All failed.

The final throw of the dice was the Rwanda plan. The idea was to fly illegal immigrants to Rwanda and process them there. My support for the bill was based on one question: would anyone pay £3,000 to cross the Channel if they thought they'd end up in Rwanda? No, they wouldn't.

Sadly, the government never got a single plane off the ground. The last attempt was stopped by activist lawyers. Then, before the policy had a second chance, an early election was called, Labour came into power, and the plan was scrapped immediately.

When we left the EU, people thought we would take back control. But staying in the European Convention of Human Rights (ECHR) prevents us from ever being truly sovereign. Any future government that wants to tackle this issue will need to have an honest conversation with the British public about leaving the ECHR.

As a side note, I'm a supporter of this idea but we must replace it with our own British Bill of Rights. Otherwise, we'll never take the public with us, and it'll be Brexit all over again. Would leaving the ECHR work? I'm not sure it's a silver bullet, but it would help. But if it is not the silver bullet, what is?

The only way we will ever stop these boats is simple: the moment they arrive, pick them up in a Chinook helicopter and fly them straight back to France. Yes, it would cause an international outcry. However, it's the only thing that would work.

The Prime Minister, whoever it is would face a barrage of condemnation from world leaders. France would be furious. There'd be tariff threats, diplomatic standoffs, and cancelled cooperation. Legal battles would follow, with endless court challenges from NGOs, activists, and possibly foreign governments. The ECHR would almost certainly be used against us. The media would erupt, both here and abroad, accusing the government of cruelty. Politicians and public figures would be vilified. Protesters would fill the streets, shouting slogans about racism and human rights. And yes, there would be short-term chaos, gridlock, backlash, and immense political pressure.

Pubs across the country would be alive with debate. Churches would condemn it. The country would be split at first. But if we held our nerve, the boats would stop. And so would the deaths.

My theory. Nobody hands over £3,000 for a dangerous sea crossing if they know they'll be flown straight back where they came from. Word would spread. Quickly too. TikTok videos glamorising life in the UK are already going viral, no wonder so many are coming. Just imagine however, a different kind of video going viral: footage of migrants being picked up by helicopter and flown straight back. That would go viral too. And far fewer would try their luck.

Would this trigger a war? Of course not. But a tariff war? Very likely. Still, as it stands, France is laughing at us. The proudest nation in Europe, being laughed at by the very country it helped liberate just 80 years ago. Shameful.

I want to address two final points and why this policy is so necessary. First, this is not about turning our backs on genuine refugees. Britain has a proud record of helping those truly in need. But most of the people arriving in small boats are not fleeing war. They've passed through multiple safe countries, France among them and are often economic migrants, not asylum seekers. That distinction matters.

Second, the financial cost is out of control. Housing, feeding, and processing tens of thousands of arrivals is costing the UK billions. Hotel bills alone are reportedly £8 million a day. That's money we could and should be spending on our own homeless, our veterans, and our crumbling public services.

Some will still ask, "Isn't there another way?" There are. But they all demand political will. We could process asylum claims offshore, as Australia does. We could digitise the system and remove failed applicants faster. We could build proper biometric databases to prevent repeat fraud. We could remove the so-called 'pull factors': hotel rooms, weekly cash cards, and endless legal delays. We must be honest though. None of it will work without a real deterrent.

One final note: most illegal arrivals are young men. And as we've seen even with legal immigration, integration can sometimes fail when people keep to their own customs rather than embracing British values. If we continue to import large numbers of people legally or illegally who do not share our values, we risk severe unrest on our own streets.

And if we continue to do nothing except pass meaningless policies, illegal arrivals will keep rising. We're already at 40,000 a year. That could soon become 60,000 or more. Criminal gangs will grow richer and bolder. Smuggling will become normalised. More people will die at sea. But without real consequences for crossing, the boats will keep coming.

As I said at the start of this chapter: kindness without discernment leads to resentment. And that is exactly where we are. The people of Britain have welcomed many asylum seekers over the years, proud that we are a safe and compassionate nation. However, when that kindness is taken advantage of, or when it is offered without due consideration by politicians who fail to see the real impact it has on the daily lives of the people they serve, it turns to resentment.

Public anger will no doubt boil over. Trust in government will collapse. Fringe movements will rise. Communities will fracture. Long term unrest in our society becomes inevitable.

You may not like the solution, but you must understand the alternative. This is a simple choice: short-term outrage or long-term collapse. We cannot keep doing nothing unless we are willing to lose our borders, our unity, and eventually our country. And I don't believe any of us want that. I'd much rather be in dispute with France than in conflict with people who now live among us.

The boats must stop. And I see no other way. We must leave the ECHR, put our own legal framework in place, and take decisive, practical action: return them the moment they arrive. This isn't about a lack of compassion. It's about control.

This entire section of the book is about law and order. And without control of our borders, we have neither.

There will be no revival without it.

Rape Gangs

It is impossible for me to discuss the major issues affecting our country and our culture without addressing the rape gangs.

This is going to be a disturbing chapter to read. It has been a difficult one to write. But what I am about to say needs to be said. My only regret is that I didn't say it sooner.

Between 2019 and 2024, during my time as an MP, I said very little on rape gangs. Not because I didn't care, but because I wasn't fully aware of the scale or detail. No letters landed on my desk. I've since asked former members of staff whether I received any relevant emails. I didn't. Yet one of my team often said these gangs had no geographical boundaries, and she always suspected something similar could be happening in Doncaster, the seat I represented.

I knew my colleague Alex Stafford, one of the MPs for Rotherham, was speaking up for these young girls. He rightly argued that victims "deserve justice and the truth above anything else" and lamented that "not one person in a position of authority has been held to account" for the Rotherham scandal.

During a landmark House of Commons debate in February 2021, Alex supported releasing the Home Office report and backed a petition for a public inquiry. He highlighted persistent failures:

That issue was swept under the carpet because it was seen as being inconvenient and not politically correct. Yet sweeping it under the carpet makes tensions and divisions worse.

I chose instead to focus on other issues I felt were also being ignored in Westminster. The indoctrination of our children with radical gender ideology. The neglect of men and boys, the decline of Christianity in public life. In addition, the devastating impact of mass immigration on towns like Doncaster. I recognise some will say these are separate debates, but in my view, the erosion of strong communities, moral clarity, and integration policies has direct consequences for safeguarding and law enforcement.

Having recently watched The Rape of Britain series, I cannot ignore this issue any longer. Through this book, I intend to address one of the most horrendous scandals in modern Britain. The rape of hundreds, if not thousands, of mainly white British girls. I make no claim that all offenders share the same background, but I do reflect the findings of official reports which identified patterns that must be confronted honestly and clearly haven't been until late.

The story starts in the early 2000s, when professionals inside Rotherham Council and South Yorkshire Police began raising concerns. In 2002, Home Office researcher Jayne Senior produced a report highlighting widespread abuse. It was suppressed, and she was sidelined. Youth worker Emma Jackson and others in safeguarding roles also tried to raise the alarm but were ignored, dismissed, or even threatened with disciplinary action.

Around 2009–2010, Tommy Robinson, (Stephen Yaxley-Lennon) began speaking publicly about Muslim grooming gangs in towns such as Luton, Derby, and Rochdale. He claimed that locals had been raising concerns for years and that the authorities and media were covering it up for fear of being accused of racism.

Between 2011 and 2012, he led protests in Rochdale and Telford. After the Rochdale convictions in May 2012, he spoke out about what he described as "targeted sexual abuse by groups of predominantly Pakistani-heritage men against white working-class girls, ignored by police for fear of being called racist." Because of his leadership of the English Defence League (EDL), many distanced themselves from him.

My acknowledgement here of Robinson's past is not an endorsement of all his actions or words; it is simply recognition that he raised this issue early when few others dared.

Later, journalist Andrew Norfolk, with full credentials intact, published a series of articles in *The Times* confirming much of what Robinson had claimed. His investigative work was meticulous, and he faced fierce pushback from those who didn't want to believe him or wanted the story buried. Norfolk died recently, but his work stands as some of the most courageous reporting of our time.

In 2013, Rotherham Metropolitan Borough Council commissioned Professor Alexis Jay. A highly experienced social worker and former Chief Social Work Adviser to the Scottish Government to conduct an independent inquiry into official failures. I have no doubt that the actions of both Robinson and Norfolk were part of the reason this inquiry finally happened.

Years of whistleblowing and media exposure had made silence impossible. The Jay Report, published in August 2014, revealed that over 1,400 girls were abused in Rotherham alone between 1997 and 2013. The details are harrowing. These girls were systematically raped by multiple Pakistani heritage men, passed around like rag dolls, plied with drink and drugs, and left to deal with the trauma alone. Many required repeated A&E treatment for injuries inflicted during the abuse. They spoke up and were ignored. While the Rotherham case is the most documented, similar patterns emerged in other towns across the country, proving this was not an isolated failure.

In 2004, Keighley MP Ann Cryer publicly warned about Asian grooming gangs targeting white girls, and she was met with accusations of racism. In 2008, Derby's Operation Retriever saw police convict a gang for grooming and abusing girls as young as twelve. A pattern that matched what would later emerge in Rotherham. In 2010 and 2011, reports of abuse in Rochdale were dismissed by social services, with victims labelled as making "lifestyle choices" until a BBC Panorama investigation shone a light on the failures.

In May 2012, nine men, mostly of Pakistani heritage were convicted in Rochdale for the rape and trafficking of girls, with the judge calling their crimes "callous, vicious and violent." In 2013, seven men in Oxford were jailed for a combined 95 years for child sex abuse and trafficking.

After the Jay Report in 2014, Operation Stovewood was launched by the National Crime Agency to investigate non-familial child sexual exploitation in Rotherham. It remains ongoing, with more than 200 suspects identified. *The Sunday Mirror* later reported that up to 1,000 victims may have been abused in Telford over a 40-year period, mirroring Rotherham's failures. In 2018, large-scale prosecutions in Newcastle and Huddersfield saw multiple gang members jailed for grooming and raping dozens of girls.

A 2020 Home Office report confirmed that most identified offenders in high-profile grooming gang cases were of Pakistani heritage and found institutional failings across the country. In 2023, the government announced a national inquiry into institutional cover-ups, police and council failures, and the cultural factors behind the reluctance to act.

There have been reforms to safeguarding law and practice since 2014, but it is vital to remember they came only after years of denial and still do not erase the failures or the ongoing risk.

The scale of abuse was horrifying enough. But the real scandal lies in the fact that so many people in positions of trust either looked away or actively avoided action.

Rotherham Metropolitan Borough Council's senior staff ignored or dismissed warnings from their own youth workers and researchers. In some cases, they silenced whistleblowers. Councillors were accused of prioritising "community cohesion" over the safety of children.

South Yorkshire Police, who seem to spend much of their time today revisiting the wrongs of their past, failed here too. They failed to investigate clear reports of rape and abuse. Victims were frequently labelled as making "lifestyle choices" rather than being treated as children at risk. Officers admitted they feared being accused of racism if they pursued predominantly Pakistani-heritage offenders. This is not speculation these concerns were recorded in official reports and witness testimony, making it a matter of record rather than opinion.

Children's Social Care departments received multiple referrals about the same girls but often did nothing. In some cases, social workers returned victims to the very men who had been abusing them.

Local NHS trusts and A&E departments treated physical injuries which could have only been caused by sexual violence. Those that treated these girls, through their records, must have known they were underage. But too often failed to trigger safeguarding protocols or alert the police. Some NHS safeguarding leads later admitted they did not escalate concerns because they "did not want to overreact."

The national government also failed. Reports reached ministers and the Home Office, but effective intervention came years too late. Successive governments failed to create mechanisms to hold local councils and police accountable when they ignored their safeguarding duties. It is worth noting that no senior figure in Rotherham Council or South Yorkshire Police lost their pension or faced criminal prosecution for these failings. An omission that still fuels public anger.

Teachers and school staff sometimes saw older men collecting girls from school gates but failed to raise alarms with safeguarding boards. Legally, they may not have been responsible beyond the school gate. But morally?

These were not isolated lapses. They were part of a pattern of deliberate avoidance, driven by fear, incompetence, and a complete absence of moral courage. And those who did speak up, often at great personal cost were too often treated as the problem, not the solution.

For example, Tommy Robinson. In 2014, he was sentenced to 18 months in prison after pleading guilty to two counts of mortgage fraud involving around £160,000, as part of a wider scheme worth £640,000. He served his sentence. I make no excuses for his offences, and I am not suggesting he should have escaped justice, but I do note the disparity in how individuals are treated.

Compare that to the collapse of several major UK banks in 2008, which wiped tens of billions from the economy, required a £137 billion public bailout, and left taxpayers with an estimated £33 billion net loss. Despite the scale of the damage, no senior UK banking executives were criminally charged. The most notable consequence was reputational. The removal of RBS chief executive Fred Goodwin's knighthood along with some regulatory reforms.

Two wrongs never make a right, but the disparity is glaring. An individual goes to prison for a six-figure fraud; those at the helm of financial institutions whose recklessness devastated much of the economy walk free.

The story continued when Robinson was later jailed for contempt of court after filming outside a trial involving similar crimes. He had been banned from doing so, and contempt of court is a serious matter but the question remains whether others in the same position would have been treated as harshly. This is not to argue against the principle of contempt laws, but to highlight concerns about consistency in enforcement.

This repeated pattern has fuelled claims of two-tier policing, where some individuals seem to face relentless pursuit while others escape scrutiny entirely. Whatever one thinks of Robinson, the fact remains: without his early warnings, much of this might still be hidden in the shadows.

The truth is finally coming out. Victims are bravely speaking up. A national inquiry is underway. Perpetrators and those who turned a blind eye are, at last, being held to account.

For many, it is too late. Some have died at the hands of these gangs. For others, the trauma will never fade. But the courage of those who spoke out from the victims themselves to the journalists, campaigners, and whistleblowers may at least help stop this happening again. And despite claims that this is now only a "historic" problem, recent convictions show the same patterns of exploitation continue in parts of the UK today.

We must make it absolutely clear: Any individual who thinks they can commit these crimes without spending the rest of their life in prison should think again. Anyone who knows it is happening should be able to speak out without fear of being called racist. That includes people of all backgrounds, the right to call out abuse should never be restricted by fear of labels.

This scandal proves the vital importance of free speech. Even if we dislike the messenger, their right and courage to speak out can be the difference between silence and justice.

This is not just about the monsters who committed these crimes. It is about the people in power who looked away. It is about a culture of cowardice, where protecting reputations mattered more than protecting children.

We cannot undo the past. But we can decide here and now that silence will never be an option again. No cultural sensitivity, no fear of labels, will ever be allowed to outweigh the safety of a child.

If this country is to have any claim to moral authority, we must show that we will defend the most vulnerable without hesitation, without compromise, and without apology.

I hope the national inquiry roots out every person involved in these failures and finally delivers justice and peace to the survivors. Anything less would be another wound to the soul of this country.

Final Word – Law and Order

Law and order are the foundation of a functioning nation, but it is also the thread that runs through every other part of society. If we can't protect people equally, apply justice fairly, and hold everyone to the same standard, the rest of our efforts will crumble.

And this is where we face one of the most uncomfortable truths of all: in recent years, we've allowed the law to be applied differently depending on who you are, what group you belong to, or what cause you champion. We have tiptoed around certain communities, excused certain crimes, and even changed the language of law to avoid offence. That doesn't create fairness it destroys it.

The next section will look at how this imbalance plays out in real life. How movements that began with good intentions have drifted into favouritism, how "equality" has been redefined into something entirely different, and how we can return to a standard that applies to all.

Because if the law is not equal for everyone, then it's not truly law at all.

Minority Groups

We can't revive a country if we're too afraid to speak plainly about what's going wrong. For too long, movements that began with good intentions have pushed far beyond their original purpose and, in doing so, have created new problems.

By raising some groups above others, we don't heal old wounds we open new ones. As we saw in the chapter on Boats, kindness without discernment doesn't unite, it breeds resentment. The result is mistrust, division, and a society more fractured than before.

A true revival means getting back to common sense. It means treating people equally, not elevating one at the expense of another. It means taking responsibility for our own actions, restoring fairness, and standing up for what's right. Even when it's unpopular.

If we want a stronger, more united nation, we must have the courage to see the truth for what it is and act on it.

Pride

The Pride movement have arguably been one of the most successful social movements of the last half century. The question is: was it a good movement or has it become deeply damaging?

Let's start at the beginning. Why did a movement of gay people need a flag? Why did they choose the rainbow? And why call the movement Pride?

There is no denying gay people were discriminated against, not just by individuals, but by society, businesses, and governments around the world. They hid their sexuality because they had no choice. Being homosexual was once a capital offence. After 1861, it became punishable by imprisonment, often with hard labour. Oscar Wilde was the most famous homosexual of the time to receive such a sentence.

Homosexual acts remained illegal in the UK until the Sexual Offences Act 1967 partially decriminalised them in private, between two consenting men over 21, in England and Wales. Before that, men could be given the "choice" between prison or chemical castration. That's not ancient history; it's within living memory for many.

Alan Turing, the World War II codebreaker in Bletchley Park who helped defeat the Nazis, was convicted in 1952 for "gross indecency." He accepted chemical castration and died by suicide two years later, aged just 41. In 2013, he was granted a posthumous royal pardon.

As you can see, there's no getting away from the fact that homosexuals were treated differently. Often cruelly by the law and by society. That is why Pride began.

As many movements, Pride chose an emblem, a flag. Gilbert Baker, the man who designed the rainbow flag, chose the rainbow for a reason. I believe he knew exactly what he was doing: deliberately picking a symbol to provoke the church. Of all the images to use, why that one?

In the Christian faith, the rainbow is a powerful symbol of God's promise never again to flood the Earth. To take that sacred image and use it to promote what the *Bible* calls sin is, to many believers, not just provocative but deeply offensive.

And what about the name Pride? It was chosen, apparently, because it is the opposite of shame. Shame is how many gay people felt and how others wanted them to feel. So, there we have the origin of the motivation, the symbol and the name.

After the first Pride marches in the early 1970s, the movement began to spread across major cities around the world. Each decade brought change.

In the 1980s, the HIV/AIDS crisis devastated the gay community, particularly in the US and UK. Governments were slow to act, so LGB communities created their own support networks. Groups like ACT UP and Lesbians and Gays Support the Miners emerged, blending activism with solidarity.

The AIDS crisis didn't just highlight injustice. It also exposed patterns of behaviour within parts of that community that many didn't want to talk about then and still don't now. That doesn't apply to everyone, and it doesn't define a person. But it was part of the reality at the time. It carried tragic consequences. The film *Philadelphia* brought this tragedy home to millions. I challenge anyone to watch it and not feel deeply moved by Tom Hanks' character and the injustice he suffers.

In 1989, the UK charity Stonewall was formed. Named after a bar in New York where gay men had long been targeted by police. Stonewall, as you will see, became one of the most successful activist groups Britain has ever known.

By the 1990s, more countries were decriminalising homosexuality. Television and film began including openly gay characters. Many will remember Colin and Barry in EastEnders. In America, Will and Grace and others made it normal to see gay characters on screen. Pride events grew in size, visibility, and sponsorship though critics began to say they had become too commercial. More about corporate image than community rights.

Many of our so-called national treasures eventually "came out." Freddie Mercury, George Michael, Elton John, to name just a few. Their talent was never in doubt, but their stories helped shift attitudes. Slowly, gay individuals were accepted not just as entertainers, but as colleagues, neighbours, and fellow citizens.

The 2000s and 2010s saw further progress. Anti-discrimination laws were passed. Civil partnerships were introduced. Then, marriage. On 29th March 2014, the first same-sex marriages took place in Britain.

Today, homosexuality is completely legal in the UK. Whether you agree with it or not (and you should be allowed to disagree, provided you treat people with the same respect you expect yourself), there are no laws treating gay people differently. They have the same rights, protections, and freedoms as anyone else.

In some countries, homosexuality is still illegal and persecuted. But in the UK, the mission was largely accomplished by 2014. Equal under the law. Socially accepted. The movement had won.

Could it have won differently? Yes. I believe the church and the movement could have found common ground. The *Bible* says we should love one another. If the church had remembered that and if the activists had understood the church's position, namely that same-sex activity goes against biblical teaching. Perhaps we could have avoided such deep division. Gay people may still have disagreed with that teaching, but the church could have responded with more understanding and care. And it's far harder to attack those who act with integrity and compassion.

The movement had won. But the movement didn't stop there. It carried on and gained astonishing influence. How? One word: Stonewall.

They got their ideology and their flag into everything. Into government to the point where a Conservative administration legalised same-sex marriage. Huge corporations proudly flew the rainbow. And as we'll explore in the chapters on Trans and DEI (Diversity, Equality and Inclusion) the influence on HR, recruitment, and procurement has been enormous.

The NHS, police, and fire services all joined in. Rainbow road crossings appeared. Emergency vehicles were wrapped in rainbow decals. Public employees now wear rainbow lanyards from council staff to civil servants, to school workers. The England women's football team wears rainbow armbands. The rainbow isn't just accepted it's promoted.

Through RSHE (Relationships, Sex, and Health Education), schools are now expected to teach about LGBTQIA+ identities. In trying to comply, many headteachers brought in materials from outside providers, often Stonewall, but also others. Some of these materials are deeply ideological.

The problem is that most teachers aren't trained in this. They're just reading scripts. Activist-written lesson plans are being read out in classrooms, unfiltered.

As an MP, I met with publishers and the then Children's Commissioner, asking them to remove some of this material. Neither acted.

Some of what I've personally seen; Swindon Council's material, for example, was explicit, to say the least. What exactly do young children need to know about what happens in the bedroom? Biology, yes. How babies are made, fine. But beyond that, I remain unconvinced.

Even with pushback from brave individuals, the movement has still flourished. Why?

Because it successfully sold the idea that to disagree is to be homophobic. And if you disagree with the T, then you're transphobic. Those labels destroy careers. They are lies but powerful ones. And they've done immense damage to freedom of speech.

Even I, as an MP, was challenged. "Words matter," I was told. Quite right and mine should count as much as anyone else's.

Anyone who dares to challenge the movement faces instant backlash. Social media mobs. HR investigations. Missed promotions. Dismissals. You name it. That's the great irony. A movement that once fought for the right to be different now condemns those who differ from it.

When same-sex marriage was achieved, the LGB movement must have celebrated. But then what? When your entire identity is built on struggle, victory can feel empty. I think some activists asked: What now? And the answer was: Trans.

The "T" joined the LGB or at least for some it did. Then came Q for queer, I for intersex, A for asexual, and finally the "+" to cover everything else. The acronym ballooned. So did the ideology. Today, the movement champions what I believe are in some cases serious mental health issues. Not treated with therapy. But with affirmation. And the results can be tragic.

Stonewall, Mermaids, PinkNews; the organisations keep growing. But the goal has shifted. It's no longer about fairness. It's about confusion. It's about forcing beliefs on others. It's about turning sexuality into celebrity. And in some deeply troubling cases, it's about giving access to vulnerable people who should be protected.

Drag queens are being invited to read to children. One local Pride event advertised a "lot of filth" their words, not mine.

Celebrities once simply 'came out' and carried on performing. Now, they promote the ideology on social media, parading their sexuality at every opportunity. Knowing full well their audience is often made up of young, impressionable fans. And it's not just LGBT celebrities; others do it too. But where are the age ratings on music videos? There are none. So, they get away with it.

I know many gay people who now want nothing to do with this movement. They didn't sign up for this. They just wanted to live in peace. And they earned that right. Many who marched in the first Pride parades now feel the movement no longer represents them. They fought for dignity and equality. Not drag queens in schools, rainbow police cars, or the erasure of biological sex.

For an entire month each year, companies, councils, broadcasters, even banks saturate their branding in rainbows. Yet the same organisations wouldn't dare celebrate free speech, marriage, or traditional values with the same intensity, if at all.

Most people were happy with a live-and-let-live approach. But the movement didn't stop there. It went from "accept us" to "affirm us" to "celebrate us, or else." That's not equality. That's coercion.

Let me be clear: this chapter is not an attack on gay people. It's a defence of free speech, parental rights, and the innocence of childhood. I recognise the battles that were fought. I respect those who just wanted to live without fear. But the movement has gone beyond fairness. It has become ideological, intrusive, and at times, oppressive. Disagreeing with that doesn't make me hateful. It makes me honest.

So, with all this progress, do we still need Pride? It fought discrimination and won. So, I would say no. The aim has been achieved. Apparently not. The movement keeps pushing and many would say, pushing too far.

It went from seeking tolerance to demanding celebration. It now divides churches, political parties, corporations, communities, and friends. It celebrates in the high street what should happen in the bedroom, and it turns on anyone who dares to question it.

This movement has rocked the foundations of society. It has attacked free speech. It has discriminated against those with opposing views. It has put sexual ideology into the textbooks of primary schools. It has made a mockery of our police force. A police officer chasing criminals in a rainbow car? Oh, please.

And it has cost the nation a fortune, supporting something that achieved its goals years ago but just won't let go. Why? Because its power no longer comes from being oppressed. It comes from being untouchable.

That's why Pride must end. Not because of hate but because we know what happens when movements forget their mission. As you'll see in the next chapter on Trans, it can lead to complete madness.

My suggested actions and a way forward come at the end of this section in the chapters on Trans and DEI. The overlap is significant, so I've left them for there. But be assured there is a way forward. And we must take those steps now.

Sometimes, you have to know when you have won. The Pride movement certainly has. There is no overall discrimination against gay people, and nor should there be.

Trans

I first heard about "Trans" when I became an MP. Until then, it had largely passed me by. I vaguely recall one of my staff explaining what it was about. I remember thinking, "What next?" But as a new MP, I had so much on my plate, it wasn't at the top of my list.

That changed. Over time, the issue kept landing in my inbox. It kept appearing on social media. I started to take a closer look at what was being put in front of me.

At first, it all seemed quite bizarre. And if it seemed bizarre to me, a sitting MP, it must you. So, let's start with what Trans is.

A trans person believes they were born in the wrong body. This is called gender dysphoria, and I do believe it exists. I understand. Gender dysphoria is a recognised psychological condition where a person feels distress due to a mismatch between their biological sex and their internal sense of gender.

It must be deeply distressing to look at your body and feel like it doesn't belong to you. They say when someone loses a limb, they can still feel it, a kind of ghost pain. Perhaps gender dysphoria is something like that: a painful mismatch between mind and body. But it is the way we're expected to treat these individuals, medically and socially, where the problems begin.

People with gender dysphoria certainly have a medical condition. But unlike a missing limb, this is a psychological issue, not a physical one. The idea we are "born in the wrong body" is false. If this is not physical, then it must be mental and should be treated as such. Counselling is the way forward. Lots of support. Understanding. But not surgery. Not puberty blockers. And certainly not everything else that followed.

As you will have been unable to avoid, the world in regard to trans went slightly mad. As I wrote in the section on Pride, I believe that, following the wins the Pride movement achieved with same-sex laws, they found themselves with a gaping hole to fill.

What next? The money pouring in and activists' staff still wanting to be activists. I believe they saw this very minuscule group of people as a way forward. A way to continue disrupting every agency from government and business to schools. Even down to the public toilets in our towns and parks. And our churches too.

And they did. As they did when lobbying for gay rights, they accused anybody who pushed back against trans as transphobic. They managed to get transgender materials into all our schools through RSHE lessons. Yes, you guessed it. Stonewall again plus others. Some respected publishers.

The activists managed to get this belief system into every university. These students become teachers, who, although they may not understand all the issues surrounding this, have been taught not to debate, not to question but to accept or you're transphobic.

Many of these influenced young people who become special advisors in government departments. They've entered HR department. They've found themselves in our NHS, in fact, all our public services and private businesses too. Just like any other generation, they've gone to work. But many have been told speak out against anything trans, and you're transphobic. So, they don't. Or at least many don't.

Many will be saying the same thing: "What's wrong with being kind?" And if you push back, "You're transphobic." I've seen transgender social workers. People with mental health issues, going into homes to help, often, people with mental health issues.–We must be able to question whether this situation is right for both parties?

Sadly, in extreme (and, I must admit, rare) cases we are seeing children taken away from parents because they won't accept that their child is trans, and that is then classed as abuse. We also see the opposite, where deluded parents think their child is "born in the wrong body" and the child is rightly removed for safeguarding reasons.

As I say later, our culture now glorifies transgender identity in the arts world, treating it as heroic, when that should not be the case. We are letting our children see this ideology on their phones, then teaching them that this is normal in our schools. And when they start to feel a little insecure or need a reason as to why they're not the most popular child in school, or they like playing with dolls instead of cars, they think, "I must be born in the wrong body."

A good parent would always want to stop this. But good advice and help can often be difficult to come by. I suppose a parent might do a little research, maybe look at a bit of history. So, let's.

Let's look back at two early figures often raised by activists. Coccinelle (1931–2006), born Jacques Dufresnoy, became a Parisian cabaret star after sex-reassignment surgery in 1958. He legally married in 1960, symbolising change in French law. He later became an activist for trans rights.

Or Lili Elbe (1882–1931), born Einar Wegener, a Danish painter who transitioned to live as Lili. Lili was one of the first to undergo multiple gender-reassignment surgeries but died after a failed uterus transplant at just 48.

This story is portrayed in the film *The Danish Girl* as a peaceful journey of self-fulfilment. The truth was much darker: medical trauma, intense emotional distress, and a life cut short.

These individuals lived at the very edge of medicine and society. They suffered. They were not "liberated." They were test cases. Even history is being rewritten to make the trans ideology work. We have an entire system, education, healthcare, media, even entertainment built around affirming this ideology without question.

I've spoken many times about backbones or rather, the lack of them. About weak leaders surrounding themselves with "yes" people. Nowhere is that more visible than in the trans debate. As I said in the chapter on politics, our public institutions are now overrun with quangos, unelected, unaccountable bodies led by careerists more worried about HR policies than the public good.

And the biggest quango of all? The NHS. An organisation that should be about health now waves more trans pride flags than anyone. In doing so, it prescribes the removal of healthy breasts and prescribes puberty blockers to children. It peddles this ideology. They may deny it, but if they fly the flag, they are endorsing it.

There is no fence-sitting for an organisation like the NHS. Wave the flag and you are "for it" and complicit in everything that follows.

A search online: "my daughter thinks she's trans." You'll land on an NHS page, but from there you're led to a range of affirming sites. One I find particularly disturbing is The Penguin Story, a cartoon image of a penguin family with the caption: "We can't always tell if you're a boy or a girl. But either way, we love you just the same." The next page says, "You can tell us later and we'll change your name, and we'll love you just the same." So kind, isn't it?

Well, ask a detransitioner. Someone who went through the puberty blockers. Went through the double mastectomy. Ask them if it feels "kind" when they look at the scars. Ask Keira Bell.

Yes, the young girl who went on this journey, had both breasts removed. Ask her if being kind was the answer. You see, that's the problem with activists. They don't really care. They just pretend to. And when it all goes wrong, they run for cover.

And she's not alone. Detransitioners are growing in number. Young people who now live with deep regret but feel silenced by the same system that once affirmed them.

And schools? I spent much of my time as an MP uncovering what was going on in classrooms. Many schools were teaching children, as fact, that they could be "born in the wrong body." Some were doing so behind parents' backs. Schools hid behind copyright laws to keep lesson materials secret. Secret from parents. What has happened to a country where what teachers are teaching our children is kept hidden from parents?

I wrote countless letters to people in power, including the Education Secretary. To her credit, she listened. Under my urging and others, she wrote twice to schools asking them to stop this madness.

But as I've explained elsewhere in this book, it's not so simple. The real power now lies with unelected ideologues in the system. People who push this agenda while simultaneously erasing Christian values from schools. Yes, ask to sing a hymn in assembly and it's "offensive." Tell a child they can change sex or choose from 76 different genders and that's perfectly fine.

I cannot speak on this subject without mentioning Disney. Simply the most despicable organisation. Once the gold standard of childhood imagination: Mickey Mouse, Snow White. Now? Nothing but a corporate Pinocchio. Except they're not a little boy. They're adults in a boardroom, poisoning the minds of their own customers.

In recent years, Disney has embraced transgender and nonbinary representation, especially in content for children and teens. They've cast trans actors in kids' shows. They've created nonbinary characters for eight-year-olds. What was once family entertainment is now activism. A move many parents didn't ask for and certainly didn't approve. And one simply thrust upon our children.

This isn't inclusion. It's indoctrination. My only hope is they see sense quickly or that the whole thing collapses, taking every board member's career with it.

Which leads me on to the workplace. We've all seen the pronouns appear. Many big businesses, many councils, telling employees to put their pronouns forward.

Sainsbury's asking staff to wear name badges with "she/her" on them. What nonsense and again, not done for compassion. They don't care. No, they just want to outdo the next weak supermarket chain in who can be the most "kind," regardless of the consequences, as long as they sell more cheap milk a farmer has to subsidise.

And it's not just happening in big business. Smaller businesses are now being asked for a DEI policies. You see, just like good practice can move down the supply chain, so can bad practice. No policy. No accreditation, no accreditation, no work. Go bust?. That's how it will work. And all the time, the real victims go unheard, hidden behind a sea of weak CEOs waving pride flags.

I mentioned Keira Bell, and that is where the real tragedy lies. Those genuinely suffering from gender dysphoria are the ones who get hurt most. They get used. Pushed down a medical path they might later regret. They deserve love. They deserve compassion. They deserve proper help not surgery, not drugs, but real counselling. Sadly, too often, they get treated like lab rats.

The Cass Review was the turning point. It found that NHS gender care for children was based on weak evidence, prioritised ideology over mental health, and rushed vulnerable young people into irreversible treatments. That's not my opinion. That's now the NHS's official conclusion. The report ended the routine use of puberty blockers and called for a cautious, holistic, psychologically informed approach to care.

Puberty blockers in children have stopped but not for all. A new £10 million clinical trial is underway in the UK. As I said: children treated as "lab rats." On our NHS.

One of the most significant areas after protecting the vulnerable is fairness in sport. I met with the Football Association in Westminster after a teenage girl broke her knee playing against a trans woman, a biological male, in a local village in my constituency. The FA waffled about hormone levels and bone density. I told them straight: if it happens again, it's on you.

You see, I believe much of this has only taken hold because of weak leaders. We've promoted people because of DEI targets, not competence. And now we have weak, confused leaders pushing this ideology at every level of society. It truly is a vicious circle.

This may sound like a rant. Maybe it is. But when I see that transgender flag, I think of the children who will never have children of their own due to puberty blockers. I think of that girl's broken knee. I think of the teenager who now regrets her mastectomy. I think of the explicit images shown to children in classrooms. And I think of my own future granddaughter (I do not have one yet) forced to share a changing room with a man suffering with mental health issues.

The legal fightback has begun. In April this year, some common sense finally arrived. The Supreme Court ruled unanimously that, in the Equality Act 2010, "sex" refers strictly to biological sex, not gender identity.

This matters. It means that while trans individuals still have protections under the Equality Act, they may now be legally excluded from single-sex spaces. And now legal action is catching up. More schools, NHS trusts, and councils will face scrutiny for putting ideology before safeguarding.

The FA moved to ban trans women from women's football in compliance with this ruling. Maybe my meeting worked because some clubs such as Goal Diggers FC chose to withdraw in protest. More fool them. I hope the courts stand firm. We shall see.

We are facing a mental health crisis. And we have schools, celebrities, and Disney normalising the idea that boys can become girls and vice versa. Why? Weak government. Weak CEOs. And well-funded activists who do not know when to stop.

We often hear people say they want to be on the "right side of history." Trust me, if you've gone along with this, you're not. I believe those who support this ideology fall into one of three groups: The weak too timid to speak up. The naïve, genuinely believe it's right. The wicked, know it's wrong, but push it anyway.

Let me end with some solutions

First, where we can, stop buying from companies that fly the transgender flag. Support anyone brave enough to push back online, in your community, wherever.

Dads and mums: Step up. Be the wall. When your child comes home talking about this? Listen. Talk. Then be firm. It's hard now, I know. But it'll be harder when your daughter's 22 and scarred by regret. See a trans flag at school? Say something. Call it out.

Schools: Stop teaching this nonsense. You know you're doing it. Stop. And stop buying lesson plans from affirming organisations, such as Stonewall. You are literally funding the confusion of the children you teach.

Business: Stop the flag-waving and cut all funding to trans organisations. I don't know anyone who buys from you because of this ideology, but I do know many who walk past because of it. Go woke, go broke isn't just a slogan; it's reality.

Quangos and sports organisations: You know what to do. Find your backbone.

Celebrities: The people who made you famous and wealthy beyond your wildest dreams are paying a huge price for your championing of this ideology. Stop. Please. Stop.

Government: If you let this continue, you'll be remembered not as leaders but as enablers, complicit in the breakdown of families, communities and our country. Yes, it is that severe. Why? Because if we as a nation cannot distinguish between a man and a woman, we are lost. Totally lost.

Government must also call out Stonewall. In my view, it has become one of the most damaging organisations in British public life.

Finally, to those genuinely struggling with gender dysphoria: I mean you no harm. I want you to get well. But if you're truly suffering, surely you don't want others to suffer like you? And I'm afraid by celebrating this condition, we are only ensuring more young people will be pulled into confusion and pain.

I'll finish as I once finished in Parliament:

"I believe that there are many bad actors who have peddled this nonsense, clearly knowing what they were doing while destroying our young people's lives. If there is any justice, those individuals should feel the full weight of the law. I hope that they are quaking in their boots. They ought to be."

— Nick Fletcher Conservative MP for Don Valley, 15th April 2024

Black Lives Matter (BLM)

I was on a train during lockdown, completely empty. I spent the journey reading, as happens on most weekdays when you're an MP.

Social media was exploding. YouTube videos were going viral. My phone was pinging every thirty seconds. America seemed to be tearing itself apart.

Why? Well, the roots of this unrest go back many years, but the immediate trigger was the death of George Floyd at the hands of a police officer.

There were many stories circulating at the time. Floyd's criminal past was being discussed, and some questioned whether he should be seen as a martyr. But that misses the point. If his death exposed deep injustices within a nation and its police force, then it served a purpose.

The court found that George Floyd's death occurred as a result of Officer Derek Chauvin's actions, without intent to kill but while committing felony assault. The officer was ruled to have acted with a "depraved mind" and without regard for human life, culpable of gross negligence that caused Floyd's death.

Chauvin is now serving a 22.5-year sentence. The Floyd family received a $27 million payout.

Was justice served? Many would say no, they wanted a much steeper sentence. Others say he was never going to receive a fair trial. An innocent verdict would likely have caused even greater civil unrest.

Police shootings in America are sadly frequent. And while more white people are shot overall, the ratio tells a different story when adjusted for population. Black Americans are disproportionately affected.

So, the real question is this: are these disparities due to race, or to poverty? And if poverty is the issue, is that itself a legacy of racism?

We don't have to look far back in history to understand why some raise these questions.

It's not many lifetimes ago that Black people were bought and sold as slaves. It hardly bears thinking about, the pain and suffering endured simply because of skin colour.

I remember watching Roots as a boy. I don't know how it was received nationally, but I remember some horrific scenes. I also recall reading how the conditions aboard slave ships were so dire that only one in five survived the journeys. Many chose to throw themselves overboard rather than continue the suffering. One chapter in the book described a belowdecks scene of 'blood and mucus, resembling a slaughterhouse.' Just picture that to understand what it might have looked like.

One of the toughest questions I've asked myself writing this book is, if I had been around at that time, would I have treated these people the same? I do hope not. But if we're honest, when something is normalised, we're all capable of blindness. I truly hope I would have seen through it. How any human being could treat another like that is beyond comprehension. But they did. I wanted to dive deeper into those stories. It would take not just a chapter, but a full book to convey the full horror of what so many men and women endured.

Slavery in the British Empire was made illegal in 1807. In 1833, it was outlawed in the British West Indies. In 1804, a slave revolt in Haiti led to an independent Black nation.

In 1863, Abraham Lincoln issued the Emancipation Proclamation, freeing enslaved people and allowing them to enlist in the Union Army. In 1865, the Thirteenth Amendment abolished slavery in the United States. Shockingly, Mauritania didn't officially abolish slavery until 1981. That's within many of our lifetimes.

Even after slavery was made illegal, the poor treatment and segregation of Black people, especially in the USA, persisted for decades.

This brings us to the civil rights movement, which emerged in the 1950s to challenge segregation, segregation that, in many places, had been enforced from the mid-19th to the mid-20th century.

You may have heard of the Jim Crow laws, which lasted from 1877 to 1954. There was no person named Jim Crow, the name came from a racist minstrel character created by Thomas Dartmouth Rice, a white performer who exaggerated Black features and mannerisms for entertainment. These caricatures were cruel and dehumanising, portraying Black people as foolish, subservient, and unintelligent.

That such a figure gave his name to a set of laws shows how deeply racism ran.

These laws enforced segregation across travel, education, housing, and public facilities. Black Americans were told they were "separate but equal" but the reality was far from equal. These laws simply gave second-class citizenship for almost a century. Slavery was over but the mistreatment of people based on skin colour continued.

I've often wondered what it must have felt like to be treated as a second-class citizen with no one to turn to. Do you stay and endure? Or try to leave? And if so where to? And how?

Many didn't run. They stood and fought for equality. And as you'll see in the next chapter, on Diversity, Equity and Inclusion (DEI) you'll understand where the push for equality came from.

These were dark times in the USA. But from them emerged bright lights. Leaders like Martin Luther King Jr.

His "I Have a Dream" speech is one of the most powerful ever delivered. The last time I heard it was at President Trump's inauguration. I've watched the full recital many times.

"I have a dream today. I have a dream that one day every valley shall be exalted, every hill and mountain shall be made low, the rough places made plain, and the crooked places made straight; and the glory of the Lord shall be revealed, and all flesh shall see it together."

This was their hope.

Martin Luther King Jr. was assassinated in 1968.

He was a Baptist minister and proof, for those who claim Christianity is a religion of oppression, that faith can lead to justice. Martin Luther King Jr., William Wilberforce, and countless others knew that in God's eyes, we are all equal.

So how did things progress?

In 1954, the Supreme Court ruled segregation in public schools unconstitutional. In 1955, Rosa Parks was arrested for refusing to give up her bus seat and once again, the courts declared the segregation law invalid. In 1957, the Governor of Arkansas used the National Guard to stop Black students entering Little Rock High School. President Eisenhower responded by sending in federal troops.

Sit-ins began at segregated lunch counters. Even children protested in what became known as the Children's Crusade. There was a bomb attack on a church, killing four young girls and injuring fourteen more. In 1963, Martin Luther King gave his 'I have a dream' speech after a march on Washington.

I recently visited Washington myself. You can feel the history. Monumental change happened there. You can almost still hear his voice echoing, "I have a dream…"

In 1964, President Lyndon B. Johnson signed the Civil Rights Act; a stronger version of what JFK had proposed before his assassination. It banned racial discrimination in employment, public facilities, and voting.

Malcolm X, another key figure, campaigned not just for civil rights, but for human rights. He was assassinated in Harlem.

In 1967, the Supreme Court struck down laws banning interracial marriage. That's just five years before I was born.

That same year saw more riots. And 1968 brought the tragic assassination of Martin Luther King Jr. Riots followed, pushing Congress to pass the Fair Housing Act, which made it illegal to deny housing based on race.

Imagine being told you couldn't marry the person you loved or buy the house you wanted because of your skin colour.

We cannot speak of the fight for Black equality without mentioning Nelson Mandela and apartheid in South Africa.

As in the USA; Black people in South Africa were treated appallingly under segregation. A resistance movement grew in the 1940s, inspired in part by America's civil rights struggle.

But unlike in the U.S., South Africa's leaders were imprisoned. Mandela himself spent 27 years in jail before becoming president in 1994. From prisoner to president. What a story.

The civil rights movement influenced much of what happened in this country. We may not have had Jim Crow laws, but we had signs in Britain that said, "No Blacks, No Dogs, No Irish." The prejudice was quieter, but it was still there.

The Equality Act 2010 strengthened many of our existing anti-discrimination laws. (It's important not to confuse this with the Human Rights Act 1998, which incorporated the European Convention on Human Rights into UK law. That is an entirely separate debate, and one I have covered elsewhere.)

The question remains, why, after all the hard-fought victories and tears of joy, did an organisation like BLM appear?

Simple, because while laws can change, hearts don't always follow. Prejudice lingers. And that's really the point of this chapter and much of this book.

Government can lead, legislate, and even inspire but it's people who must truly change. Some people may not want to change. But for those who do, we should still be able to talk about each other's heritage without fear or scorn. We should make room for honest questions, even when they're clumsy or uneducated, and respond with grace rather than outrage. We should allow for each other's ignorance and educate one another.

Sadly, much of the ideology behind Black Lives Matter stems from Critical Race Theory, an academic 'framework' that views society is inherently structured to benefit white people at the expense of others.

While this theory began in universities, it has crept into schools, HR departments, and even police training. It teaches that racism isn't just personal prejudice but embedded in systems and that only radical change can fix it.

I believe this approach divides rather than unites us. It shuts down the very dialogue that could build bridges by branding every poorly worded question as racism, rather than an opportunity to connect.

The riots following George Floyd's death may have set race relations back years. The looting, arson, and violence damaged the cause. Toppling statues, removing poems from universities, none of that helps.

We shouldn't celebrate slave traders but erasing history means erasing the chance to learn.

One of the most infamous 'statue topplings' was that of Edward Colston in Bristol. He made a fortune from the slave trade yet bizarrely was also a philanthropist who funded schools and hospitals. Was this out of guilt? Or did he simply not see the wrong, as it was normalised in his day? Either way, I understand the anger. But toppling every platform from history doesn't help us learn. I'm pleased he can still be viewed as a reminder of what not to do, now displayed at Bristol's M Shed museum.

Worse still, it sets a precedent: when you disagree, riot. Boarding up Winston Churchill's statue was a sad day. Without him, this country and much of the world would be a very different place.

There's another danger too. If we don't treat each other's history with respect, and if we assume past wrongs justify present revenge, we tip the scales again. Instead of equality for all, we risk inequality in reverse.

This brings me to "taking the knee." They say it's a sign of respect. But I believe we should only kneel before God. I knelt twice for my wife; it's a longer story and I would kneel for the King. But beyond that, no. If we kneel for others, where does that leave equality? The pendulum has swung too far.

In addition to the kneeling campaign, the BLM movement also pushed the slogan "Defund the Police." I'm not sure who thought that would gain public support, but it quite clearly didn't.

When cultures clash, and racism is suspected rightly or wrongly, it doesn't take much to reignite old tensions. That's why I hope this chapter helps. Understanding past wrongs, acknowledging how far we've come, and remembering that no one is born racist. We are taught.

We must therefore always be the best role models for the next generation. Legislation can help, but a good heart is what will truly conquer division, no matter how it manifests.

Forgiving nations for past wrongs, even when those responsible are long gone is difficult. Which brings me to reparations.

These are payments or assistance given to make amends for past injustices. While the idea may sound good to some, in theory, in practice it is unworkable. Who pays? How much? For how long? To whom?

In reality, the money would come from you and me. And sadly, in many nations, it would never reach those it's meant to help.

The best way to support former colonies or struggling nations is through free trade, good relationships, shared ideas, and mutual inspiration. When done right, capitalism means one person's success doesn't come at someone else's expense. It means everyone can benefit. It follows that when one nation prospers, others can too. Let's be good neighbours. But let's not bankrupt ourselves in the process. That's not how true equality works.

I think we can see why people of colour had cause to be angry but the way that anger was expressed did neither the movement nor the cause much good.

To the question, are the disparities felt by the Black community due to race or to poverty? And if poverty is the issue, is that itself a legacy of racism? I think the answer is yes to both.

Racism existed. It no doubt caused poverty. And poverty, in turn, causes disparities. But the laws have changed. And many people of colour have outperformed many white people.

Too often, movements like BLM and theories such as CRT divide rather than unite, framing society in terms of victims and oppressors instead of building a common path forward.

The only way forward is treating everyone as equal. Treating one another with respect. Forgiving past wrongs, however far back we must go. Remembering the lessons of history, not erasing them. And building a future set firmly on Christian principles, loving your neighbour as yourself.

Diversity, Equality and Inclusion (DEI)

Diversity, Equality and Inclusion (DEI) is one of the most damaging policies of the 21st century. It's another example of the "be kind" culture, where we're no longer allowed to say no. The idea behind DEI is to avoid discrimination based on "protected characteristics" including age, disability, gender reassignment, marriage, civil partnership, pregnancy and maternity, race, religion or belief, sex, and sexual orientation. And the list keeps growing. Let us take a quick look at where all this started and why it was thought to be needed.

Sadly, I believe our greatest ally the USA has often exported some of our worst imports. Most agree that DEI began in the mid-20th century, which led to the Civil Rights Act of 1964. This act in America rightly aimed to tackle segregation and racial injustice, as we've just read in the chapter on BLM. But over time, what started as a noble effort gave way to hiring people to meet quotas, not merit-based hiring, but identity-based selection. And like many American ideologies, it didn't stop at the border.

Would anyone genuinely want to discriminate based on these traits? Sadly, as we've seen, yes. Some still look down on people of colour. Some men still look down on women. But there are also many who hold hostility toward men, and I've encountered some of them, particularly in Parliament, ironically the supposed home of democracy.

Discrimination based on race still exists. It is wrong, but it's a reality. Yet it also cuts both ways. In many parts of the world, white people are now experiencing hostility and, in some cases, violence purely because of their skin colour. We've also seen the historic and ongoing persecution of people based on their faith.

DEI was meant to protect against this yet here in the UK, Christians are being targeted by our own Parliament. Silent prayer in public is now, as we saw in the chapter on abortion, considered illegal. The "kindness" brigade argues this is to protect women near abortion clinics, and while there are valid points on both sides, we must recognise the broader trend.

So where does this lead us? Surely the law should protect us from such harms.

In theory, yes. But as a true conservative, I believe in personal responsibility. We should govern ourselves, not rely on overbearing laws to do it for us.

Let me give you an example. Take the N-word. I detest it, and I hope most people do too. But I haven't heard it used in decades not because of the law, but because society has decided it's unacceptable. That's self-governance in action.

Yet as a Christian, I hear blasphemy almost daily. The name of Jesus used as a swear word, sacred phrases thrown around casually. These too are offensive to many yet completely tolerated. If DEI were truly about equality, shouldn't both forms of offence be treated the same? This double standard proves that we don't need state-enforced kindness, we need mutual respect, applied fairly.

In my workplace, I don't hear that kind of language, because I don't allow it. I don't hear it at home or in my car. And my friends respect me enough not to use it. That's mutual respect. That's personal responsibility.

So, if we can self-govern in some areas, why not in all? Why do we need laws telling us to value one group over another? Where does it stop?

It's become a minefield. Discrimination lawsuits are common, and DEI has arguably gone too far in trying to solve the issue. I return to the idea that kindness without discernment creates resentment. We're seeing growing frustration towards individuals who appear to be hired or promoted as part of a box-ticking exercise rather than on merit. Companies boast about DEI compliance while their brands decline, sales drop, and profits are swallowed up by endless red tape.

Here's another example: when an employer hires mostly one demographic, no one complains. No one 'bats an eyelid' when an Indian restaurant hires an all-Asian staff. Should they be required to hire only 9.3% Asian workers to match the national average? Of course not. In Parliament, during the 2019–2024 term, there were at least 60 MPs identifying as gay, yet that's well above the national average. Should we remove 40 MPs to balance the stats? Of course not.

So why is overrepresentation in favour of a "protected" characteristic fine, but underrepresentation sparks outrage?

We've created a culture of victim mentality; a mindset built on blame. Always somebody else's fault, never our own.

Some activists argue, 'I didn't get on, so it must be discrimination.'

Others insist, 'I didn't get promoted, so bias must be to blame.

Too many activist organisations who say they are supporting minority groups have come to rely on this as their foundation, even managing to push themselves into key positions in institutions that once prized meritocracy. DEI is now taking over.

If a bad employer refuses to hire someone because they're black, gay, or disabled, they're not just breaking the law, they're missing out on talent. But the same is true in reverse. If a business hires someone just because they tick a diversity box, and not because they're the best person for the job, they could also be losing out.

What if we started seeing the straight, white, able-bodied Christian, who often feels sidelined, get a role not because of their merit, but because society has started to kick back against DEI? Where's the value in that? Whether it's exclusion or overcompensation, the result is the same: you've hired based on identity, not ability. And in the end, the worm eats itself.

The only way a person, a business, or a country can truly grow is through merit. And recognising merit can only come through truth. Nothing else will last.

DEI is also affecting those who have not even started in the workplace. It is recognised that white working-class boys are achieving less and often ending up costing the state rather than contributing to it. Why? Because we seem unable to help girls without also helping boys. We can't support black or Asian students without overlooking the struggling white working-class boy at the back of the classroom, who just needs a little push.

Is this because the white working-class kid has so-called white privilege? Or is it because we're selecting teachers using DEI quotas? I genuinely don't know. But if DEI is running rife through some of the biggest private sector companies and we know it's running rife in the NHS, why would schools be any different? Again, is DEI causing a problem because of

DEI? I don't know. But I do know this: weak leaders often buckle under activist pressure. And school heads are leaders.

Another industry that was about to be dealt a DEI nightmare was the financial services sector via its regulator, the FCA (Financial Conduct Authority). During my time in Parliament, the FCA was preparing to impose DEI quotas across the financial sector pressuring firms to hire based on identity, not merit.

Can you imagine entrusting your life savings to a financial adviser who got the job because of a DEI quota and then you lost everything? I was involved in efforts to stop it. Alongside others, I pushed back, making it clear that Britain's businesses must be free to choose the best person for the job, not the most "diverse" candidate on paper. In March 2025, the FCA withdrew its proposal. It was a small but significant victory for common sense, and a reminder that we can reverse this agenda when we have the backbone to stand up to it.

And the truly sad part? For individuals who would have risen to the top on merit, DEI casts a shadow. It creates doubt.

Imagine a woman who has worked her way up the career ladder. She's put in the hours, gone the extra mile. Night classes. Hard graft. All while raising a family and making a home. And when she finally lands the top job, someone says she only got it because of company policy.

That is deeply damaging.

Yes, it's wrong when someone is denied a job because of racism or sexism, especially when weak individuals allow it to continue unchallenged. But it's just as damaging when DEI is so deeply embedded that even the right decisions are brought into question.

I remember speaking out in Parliament about issues facing boys and being invited onto Woman's Hour. I reluctantly agreed. When I arrived, I was taken to the third or fourth floor by a woman. I entered a room where six or seven young women were working away. In the studio, the producer was a woman. The interviewer, Nuala McGovern, a woman. I think the interview went well. But even then, I wasn't brave enough to ask, where were the men?

The BBC probably champions diversity more than any other organisation. Yet that room was all female. Now, Nuala is very good at what she does that's not in doubt. But I never asked whether she got her job because she was the best candidate or because she was a woman. Can you imagine if I had? I doubt I'd have got out of there alive.

And that's the dilemma DEI creates. Everyone there may well have been the best person for the job and I hope they were. Yet the question now lingers where once it would never have existed.

It also influences free speech. Whistle-blowers feel unable to call out poor performance or bad behaviour because the individual ticks a DEI box. People are afraid to say no to a Pride lanyard because it goes against their faith. Refusing to add pronouns to an email signature can now put your job at risk. DEI appears to work against everything instead of for everything.

It's not only bad for employment, bad for individuals, and bad for productivity, it's also bad for profit. Huge departments are now set up to deal with this nonsense. If private companies want to spend their money and watch their profits fall, that's their lookout. But when it's taxpayers' money, surely, we should have a say.

Another example where DEI is working against men is in the courts. In most custody cases, it's mum who gets the kids. Where is the inclusion in that policy? When it works for a supposedly excluded identity, this time, women, no one complains. Now, I know in many cases mum is best placed. But instead of a starting position of 50/50 childcare, we begin with it stacked against dad. DEI should never allow that kind of imbalance, but it's never even questioned.

The corporate world's answer to many DEI questions is that our decisions are shaped by "unconscious bias." HR firms run online courses where it's always the same story: a white man doing something wrong in the workplace, a black woman suffering because of it, a black man being passed over by a white CEO whose friend plays golf at the same club. We've all seen it, if not in person, then in policy. And yes, these things do happen. But to paint all white men as racist or sexist is not the answer. Call it out when it happens, yes. But assume parity first.

So, what's the answer? Scrap DEI. It's that simple and very easy to apply.

If employees believe they're working for a racist company or a sexist boss, they can and should just leave or at least call it out. The laws are there already. But putting so many of us in boxes labelled with an identity we can do nothing about and pitting us against each other based not on merit but on quotas, is not the way forward.

Let all of us base our decisions on an individual's character, work ethic, and competence. That's how we should choose our friends, promote our staff, and treat one another. We should be brave enough to call out nonsense and, as the *Bible* says, treat others as we would want to be treated ourselves.

It says "love one another" but I'll save that for another book. Love in the workplace might cause more problems than it solves.

Final Word – Minority Groups

I hope we have seen the division that elevating minority groups above others can cause. And that the health of a nation is not measured by how loudly it celebrates certain groups, but by how fairly it treats all its citizens.

When some are elevated at the expense of others, resentment grows, unity fades, and trust in our institutions erodes. That is not equality; it is a new form of division.

If we want true equality, we must strip away the labels and see the individual in front of us: their character, their education, their skills, their ability to do the task at hand.

And where is character formed? In the family home. It is there that values are first taught, respect is first modelled, and personal responsibility is first learned.

The next section turns to that most basic building block of society: the family. If we get that right, many of today's divisions will start to fade. If we get it wrong, no amount of political tinkering will put it right.

Family

Family is the place where our young people are formed, supported, and made ready for the world. If we get family right, we give the next generation a fighting chance in education, in work, in relationships, in life itself. If we get it wrong, no amount of government spending, school reform, or community projects will fix the damage.

When I look at Britain today, I see a nation that has slowly chipped away at its own foundations. We've made it easier to walk away from commitments, undermined the value of marriage, pushed parents to put career before children, and stripped away the value of fathers in their sons' and daughters' lives.

We have told boys they're a problem, men that they're failing, mums that they must do it all, and grandparents that their wisdom is outdated. Then we wonder why so many people are lost, lonely, and looking for meaning.

This section isn't about turning back the clock. It's about recognising that strong families in whatever form they take when built on love, commitment, and responsibility are the single greatest asset any country can have.

It's about valuing men without diminishing women. Lifting boys without neglecting girls. Supporting marriage without condemning the single or childless. Championing parenting as the most important job you will ever have. And understanding that role models matter because someone is always watching, learning, and copying.

If Britain is to have a revival, it must start at home. That means strengthening families the very place where character is formed, faith is nurtured, and values are passed down. Strong families build strong communities and strong communities build a strong country.

Men

In the UK 14 men a day are taking their own life. Just read that sentence again…

It's bad, isn't it? The thought that 14 men every single day believe the only way forward is to end their life. And what's worse? This number has risen since last year. The problem isn't getting better, it's getting worse.

Other statistics are poor too. 94% of individuals in prison are men, that's around 90,000 men. Thirty-three men a day are dying from prostate cancer. One in five men does not reach the age of 65. In one night in August 2024, 3,800 plus men were rough sleeping. So, we have to ask: why?

Like most complex problems in society, there's no single issue and no silver bullet. But there are causes, and there are solutions, if we're brave enough to look for them.

Let's go back 50 years and look at how the world and a man's place in it has changed.

Once upon a time, a man's role was clear. He was the breadwinner. He went to work. Mum often stayed at home. That gave a man identity, purpose, and value. He knew what was expected of him. Some men climbed the career ladder, but for most, simply getting up and going to work was enough. Overtime or a side hustle might have helped bring in a little more, but fundamentally, that was the job, and he did it.

Outside of work, they kept themselves entertained through local sports teams or community clubs. They fixed their cars, washed them, kept the garden tidy. Nothing fancy, just enough not to be an embarrassment to a neighbour. And for most, that life was enough.

Occasionally that breadwinner role was taken away through redundancy or sickness, it often hit hard. Not being able to provide for the family? For many men, that was unbearable. They were quick to get back to work.

Fast forward to today. In many ways, things have changed, but in others, they haven't. Many men still see providing as their duty, even though women are more likely to be in full-time work now. On paper, that should reduce the pressure, but it doesn't. In a world where two incomes are needed just to keep up with the rising cost of living, if a man loses his job, the pressure often increases. And it's made worse if he sees his partner picking up the financial slack. Even today, many men still carry that deep sense of obligation to provide.

When domestic labour-saving devices helped women go to work. Many similar devices or services took the value away from men. Men used to service the family car. Most cars are so complicated this job is almost out of reach for most men these days. Gardens are smaller. Many items are 'throwaway' and easily replaced. Even the car is washed by someone else.

Now I'm taking this further than I probably should, but you see where the man's role has been diminished, and the woman's has increased. They are now at least half the breadwinner and still often the homemaker too. This has sadly left many women doing too much and men not feeling as though they can help. Which leads me onto masculinity.

I do not like the phrase "toxic masculinity", so I won't use it again. But it can have two meanings. Firstly, it can mean basically that men and masculinity are bad and always negative against women. Another meaning is that 'feeling masculine' can influence the way a man should or should not feel. Both are bad in their own way.

Obviously, any man using his masculinity in a negative way against a partner, a work colleague, or simply women in general can have a huge effect on the way women can feel and the way they are treated. Treating anyone negatively because of their sex is not good in either direction, but with men often seen as the more powerful sex, this can be seriously damaging as we have seen in many cases across the country, in fact, across the world.

Regarding men not being able to show their feelings, this is true of so many men, me included. I was brought up that men don't cry, and I get that. But when they keep their feelings so close that their loved ones don't see this, this is where problems can occur. Men should be able to have conversations at home and in private at work without the concern of embarrassment if the feelings become overwhelming.

Sadly, I believe too many men don't feel that they can. Often this gets to a tipping point before anyone realises there is an issue. In the direst cases, it can end up being one of the statistics I started this chapter with.

I also want to touch on another issue that often goes unnoticed: the negative behaviour for which many men have rightly been called out, but which is rarely challenged when it happens the other way around.

When we simply look at the physical size of men compared to women, we think the bad behaviour can only go one way. But trust me, it can and often does, go the other way too. Many men are in abusive relationships and face bullying from female partners.

Here, masculinity works against men two-fold. One: they can never hit back and shouldn't. But they often feel too ashamed to call out the bullying from a female partner or supervisor for the fear of being laughed at. No, men can suffer just as much as women sometimes, and because of the negative look, they often suffer in silence much longer than they should.

Then there's fatherhood. I've seen firsthand the despair some men face when separated from their children. The divorce rate is high, and even though the official numbers show a decline, that's largely because fewer people are getting married. More people live together unmarried, and when those relationships break down, they aren't recorded as divorces. But for fathers, married or cohabiting, the pain of losing daily contact with their children is just as real. The result? Isolation. Despair. And financial hardship.

There are other factors too. Society has rightly fought for equality for women, people of colour, people with disabilities. But in doing so, a growing number of men feel left behind or worse, actively excluded.

Online, you'll even find viral videos where people are asked, "What are men good for?" and the reply is, "Nothing." How do you think that lands with someone who's already struggling?

As we saw in the chapter on DEI, many men feel that they're being passed over, not because they're underperforming, but because they're the wrong demographic. Whether that's true or not, the perception alone creates resentment, alienation, and hopelessness.

Health is another big issue. Men are notoriously bad at looking after themselves, especially while working. They often struggle with time off work to see a GP and let problems develop. This is often due to the manual work men do. Somehow office staff can often seem less missed (me included) but when the plumber is sick, that leak doesn't get fixed and that customer is not happy.

When men retire, they often find more time, but by then it can be too late. Men are more likely than women to suffer from obesity, alcoholism, and drug abuse, all of which are linked to suicide.

After much work from myself and others, we managed to get a men's task and finish group organised with the Department of Health. Sadly, an election was called and much of this work remained incomplete.

However, the new government has brought in a Men's Health Strategy, another issue I campaigned for, which I hope will help. Much will depend on how this is led and whether it receives any support or scrutiny from the current administration or is it simply another box-ticking exercise?

I have spoken much throughout this book of personal responsibility, but government can play its part. However, when government ministers often blame men for everything, which some do, it doesn't help much.

With regard to the atrocious murder of Sarah Everard. Instead of using her murder as a wake-up call to ask what the heck is going wrong in some men's minds to commit such a horrific crime. It sparked a barrage of hostility towards men as a whole, including ludicrous calls, from the Green Party for a 6pm curfew for men. Let me take you back to that dreadful incident.

Sarah Everard was a 33-year-old marketing executive living in London. On the evening of 3 March 2021, she disappeared while walking home from a friend's house in Clapham. She took a well-lit route and was dressed brightly. Her disappearance sparked nationwide concern and a huge police operation.

It turned out she had been abducted, raped, and murdered by Wayne Couzens, a serving Metropolitan Police officer. He used his warrant card and handcuffs to falsely arrest her under the pretence of breaking COVID rules. He then drove her to Kent, where he committed his horrific crimes and later burned her body to destroy evidence.

Couzens was arrested on 9 March and later pleaded guilty. In September 2021, he was sentenced to a whole-life term, meaning he will never be released.

Sarah's murder horrified the nation, not just because of its brutality, but because the killer was a police officer. The case triggered vigils, protests, and a flood of conversations about women's safety.

And then came the backlash, not just at Couzens or at the Met's failures, but at men in general.

One Green Party peer, Baroness Jenny Jones, suggested introducing a 6pm curfew for all men. She said:

"I would argue that at the next opportunity for any bill that's appropriate, I might actually put in an amendment to create a curfew for men on the streets after 6pm… I feel this would make women a lot safer, and discrimination of all kinds would be lessened."

What could and should have been a national moment of reckoning about how such wickedness forms in the first place was instead used to push the usual narrative: that all men are dangerous, misogynistic, and the only answer is to restrict their freedom.

Countless MPs, Mayors, Chief Constables and activists, lined up to promise and campaign for tougher sentences and more education for men about misogyny. More CCTV. Better street lighting. More police patrols. But very few dared ask the deeper question: why are some men becoming this way in the first place?

This may be one of the most controversial chapters in this book, but I think it's important to say: we all want the same thing. Every decent man wants the women he loves, his daughter, his wife, his sister, his mum, to feel safe walking home at night.

But where some propose curfews, bans, and blanket suspicion, I believe the answer lies in understanding what's going wrong and how we stop it before it starts.

Because let's be honest: if young men are constantly ridiculed, told they have no value, passed over at work, stripped of purpose, and fleeced in family courts, it's inevitable that some will spiral into bitterness or hatred. Not on the abhorrent scale of a Wayne Couzens but it will lead to other young men going down a wrong path.

No, it doesn't excuse wickedness. But if we refuse to even look at the causes, how can we ever hope to prevent the consequences?

Maybe what we need isn't just brighter lights, CCTV and louder slogans, maybe what we need is a new approach. One rooted not in blame, but in understanding. Not in silencing men, but in helping them become better men. Society has changed the role of men and if no one speaks up for them, there will be those that turn into something so evil that they carry out heinous crimes. We need a different tack.

Unfortunately, while we continue to tell them they have no value, ridicule them, and mock anyone who dares stand up for them, we reinforce the problem.

We must start to appreciate that the role of men has changed, and many struggle to deal with it. When men lose their value, they often lose their voice too. Sadly, this has left many men unable to speak up for injustices, not just against themselves but also when protecting their sons and daughters.

Obviously, this is not all men. But as we see with many who suffer with depression, the lack of confidence or the ability to ask for help creates even more depression, leading to another statistic that I started this chapter with.

There is help out there and as is often the case, it comes from the voluntary sector. The explosion in the popularity of Andy's Man Club has proved the need. I've had the privilege of attending some of these meetings. Listening to men who have often been silenced, speaking up for the first time, is a joy to be part of. The stories are often the same: redundancy, separation, inability to see their children, reliance on drugs legal and illegal to get through the day. And now, they can finally offload this.

The Samaritans is a wonderful organisation and is so needed. But Andy's Man Club is different. It gets men out of their homes. They get to share with other men going through the same issues. There's no professional counselling, just a friendly ear. But unlike other organisations that help via a phone, Andy's Man Club helps create long-lasting friendships. You see, we don't always need valuing for what we give to a relationship in function or finances. Sometimes, just being a friend to someone in need gives us enough value to push on ourselves.

There are different stages in men feeling bad about themselves and undervalued, and I believe Men's Sheds maybe offers what Andy's Man Club does but at an earlier stage. I always got the impression that by involving men in making something, and talking, it stopped them ever getting to that point of despair. I may be wrong. Either way, both are great and prove the point: when men are given something they can do to help themselves, many do. They just sometimes need the chance and maybe a little push from a government message, a workplace, or even a relative.

As I state in the chapter on boys, I have championed the need for a Minister for Men and Boys. It is needed. And one day, when certain individuals in Parliament stop using men as something to blame for all the world's wrongs, they may put a Minister for Men and Boys in place. Lift our men up, as I believe we should.

I must ask at this point two things of our wives and partners.

First, speak well of the man in your life. Not all, but many, speak down to and ill of their partner. Don't. There will come a time when you want him to be a man. And if all you have done is ridicule him, don't be surprised when he cannot be what you want him to be.

Second, if your marriage has broken down, please do not be persuaded into claiming your partner was abusive if he wasn't, simply to secure free Legal Aid. The result is devastating for all. Little Johnny doesn't see his dad. He grows up with no male role model, feels useless, and turns to the internet where he finds only a world of grievances. He becomes a man with no value, no voice, and ends up as another statistic.

To finish, to the men who are reading this be strong and proud and grab life with both hands.

You might not get cheered on. You might not see yourself reflected in diversity campaigns. You might not be the subject of documentaries or international days of awareness, aside from one token day in November. But you matter just the same.

To the man working two jobs to provide for his kids, thank you.

To the man quietly grieving a loss no one knows about, hang in there.

To the father fighting for access to see your children, don't give up. Trust me they love you.

To the young man trying to find his place in the world, keep going. It's hard but worth it. As are you.

And remember, whatever society has taught you: you are not a problem to be fixed. You are not toxic by default. You are not disposable. You are needed. You are capable. And you are loved, even if the world doesn't always say it.

This chapter isn't an excuse for bad behaviour. It's a plea to take men seriously, to understand the pressures they face, to stop blaming them for everything, and to help them find their place again in a fast-changing world.

Because when men are strong, families are stronger. Communities are stronger. The country is stronger. This isn't about turning back the clock. It's about building a future where men are valued again not for what they used to be, but for what they still are and can be.

The sooner we stop tearing men down, the sooner we'll start lifting society up.

Boys

"A dad in the home is like an alarm box on the house; it doesn't stop every criminal, but it does say: go elsewhere, someone cares here."

We have a problem. One that can be fixed, but only if someone is willing to take the lead. We need a Minister for Men and Boys. And we need one now.

I've covered men in the previous chapter, but the need for a Minister for Men and Boys, especially for our boys, is urgent. This is something that can and should be put in place without delay.

Boys become men. That's a simple fact, but one many seem to have forgotten. If we don't look after our men and help them become the examples we want for the next generation, we don't stand much chance with our boys.

The role of men in society has changed, as I discussed earlier, and that change affects our boys. That change can be positive or negative like all change, it depends how we handle it. So we must ensure the effect is positive.

When I was in Parliament, I spent a lot of time working on this subject. One woman who made a lasting impression on me was Sonia Shaljean, who runs a charity called Lads Need Dads. I can't think of a better phrase when it comes to our boys.

Yes, boys need both mums and dads. But just as I believe girls need more of their mum, I believe lads need more of their dad. Sadly, because of separation and divorce, dads are becoming increasingly absent from their sons' lives.

So, who is the man in a young boy's life? Far too often, no one. In too many cases, it's mum trying to fill both roles. Warren Farrell described single mums as among the most overworked, overwhelmed people in society, and he's not far wrong.

We can't always stop parents from breaking up. We can try and hopefully my chapter on marriage stresses how important it is but when breakups do happen, we must ensure there's still a man in that little boy's life. Preferably dad. In fact, always dad unless there's a serious safety concern.

But where that's not possible, we must actively seek the next best male role model. Grandad, uncle, trusted friend, stepdad, it doesn't matter who, so long as that boy has a man in his life who cares and shows up.

Too often, good fathers feel pushed out by a family court system that appears to favour mothers, even when dads are desperate to stay involved. That needs to change.

Parents must work with schools, and schools must be interested. A lot is expected of schools these days, and I don't always agree with that. Parents should bring up kids. Teachers should teach. Of course, there's always going to be some overlap, but schools should not be doing what a parent should do. However, they should at least be aware of what's going on at home.

If there's no father or male role model, then the school should do its best to help. That could mean identifying a mentor, a teacher, a support assistant, maybe even a sixth-former. Because if a boy doesn't have a role model, he'll go out and find one. And it may not be someone we'd choose.

This is even more vital when we consider how boys are doing in school. Today, boys are falling behind girls at almost every stage of education. They're more likely to be excluded, less likely to go to university, and far less likely to be taught by male teachers, especially in primary schools. This matters. Because boys need to see who they can become.

Once a role model is in place, they must engage properly. Not just sit on an iPad with them. They need to do something with them. A kickabout in the park. Something practical. If it must be a PlayStation session, so be it but use that time to talk. Ask about their week. Talk about next week. Discuss goals, even small ones. Celebrate the little wins and help them set new ones.

A father-son relationship takes work. It isn't always natural. Relationships between boys and male mentors outside the family take even more effort. Trust must be earned over time, and it can be lost in an instant. So be slow, steady, and honourable.

It's hard work. But the rewards are enormous, not just for the boy, not just for the mentor, but for society as a whole.

I know I sometimes write like I have all the answers. I haven't. I didn't do a bad job as a dad, but I could have done better. I was always busy, always working, always chasing the next opportunity. I thought I was doing it for the family. And I was. But I was doing it for Nick Fletcher too and I could have made more time. If I had my time again, I would.

Yes, I believe dads should work hard and be examples to their sons. But working 80 hours a week, seven days a week, is not the example we should be setting.

It's said, "A wise man learns from his mistakes." But a wiser man learns from someone else's. Please be the wiser man.

I have written a full chapter on the importance of sport and community groups. Finding something lads and dads can enjoy together is critical. It doesn't have to cost the earth. Often it costs nothing, just a little time. Whatever it is, a joint interest in something can fill hours of talking and build relationships that last. Shared interests are what create friendships. Children need the same.

I'm no fan of computer games, mostly because I've always been useless at them but if it's something a young lad loves, better to join him than leave him. You never know, you might get good.

Habits formed young are very hard to break. Keeping fit together is another brilliant thing to do. When you've spent your childhood running with your dad, it's hard to take up smoking or vaping. When you know a McDonald's is a once-a-month treat, it's hard for that to become a daily routine later on.

Kids also like routine, doing the same thing at the same time. Saturday, we watch the football. Sunday, we watch the Grand Prix. Monday, Wednesday, and Friday we go for a run. Last Friday of the month, we go to the pictures. These habits build strong relationships. So, when things get tough and influencers come along who want to pull them off course, you've already built that strong connection and it's much harder for anyone else to break in.

Kids also love tradition. Christmas morning, we do this. Birthdays, we do that. Bank holidays, we go here. These rituals again help to build that strong bond and they'll carry these traditions on with their own kids too. A strong thread running through your family line.

Much of this applies to girls as well, and I don't want anyone to think otherwise. But sadly, it is boys who seem to be struggling more, hence this chapter. However, as with all my work on men and boys, the aim has never been to help them alone, but to help everyone. When boys grow into better men, they become better partners, fathers, colleagues, and friends and that benefits girls and women too.

These ideas help build relationships that will stand the test of time. But they also help us fend off trouble in the first place. Once you have that relationship in place, you can set rules and that matters. I'll speak more about this in my parenting chapter, but it's vital that everyone, especially those with young kids or planning to have them understands this:

Kids subconsciously love rules.

Why? Because they love having someone to blame. When temptations come and they will, they need someone else to take the heat. It's not just kids. I've seen adults do it too. From the apprentice to the employee, to the CEO, to the politician, everyone looks for someone to blame. And while that's sometimes-poor behaviour in adults, it can be very useful in kids.

A young lad saying "No, my dad would go mad" is brilliant. It gives him an out. It keeps him safe. It helps him walk away from poor decisions. If we don't get this right, what happens?

I also believe we all need someone to please. We all want to be noticed. The millions of people glued to their phones, waiting for a like or a share, prove that point. We want to be seen. We want approval. We want to make someone proud and if we have no one, we will find someone.

That's why it's vital we ensure our boys have the right people in their lives, people who care, guide, protect, and believe in them.

If a boy doesn't have someone to please who cares about him, he may very well end up trying to please someone who doesn't. And those people know exactly who to target.

They know the solitary walk home from school. They see the sad, lonely boy on the street. They notice the unkempt house where dad isn't around. They are predators.

They build trust just like we hope dads, uncles, and youth workers do but their intentions are wicked. They don't care for our boys. They want to use them, abuse them, and drag them into a world of crime and misery.

As I said at the beginning "A dad in the home is like an alarm box on the house, it doesn't stop every criminal, but it does say: go elsewhere, someone cares here."
Let me finish with a true story.

I was once asked to call a lady who wanted to talk about her son. I phoned her. She answered softly:

"I'm not sure what you can do. It's probably too late for my son. But if you can help others, please do."

She paused, then said:

"Can you stop the drugs?"

As an MP, I had learned to listen. So, I did. I let her speak.

She told me her boy was a lovely lad. "Really bonnie," she said. "Would do anything for me. He loved his mum."

But something had gone wrong. He met the wrong people. Fell into the wrong crowd. Now, she said, "he's skin and bones…he smells, dresses poorly…I barely recognise him. I don't trust him anymore. He only ever comes for money."

Then, with pain in her voice:

"I'm afraid of him. He steals from me. He wouldn't hurt me…well, he might."

It was heartbreaking. This was her own son. Her flesh and blood.

She said the dad had left years ago and maybe that was the root of it.

"I blame myself," she said.

She repeated: "Just stop the drugs."

I had tears in my eyes. I told her I'd do all I could. I've since written a book on role models and distributed it to every secondary school. I posted it online. I spoke in Parliament. But it never felt like enough.

"I'm waiting for that phone call," she said finally.
"The one that tells me he's gone."

I knew the call she meant. I told her I would pray for him that night. I'll pray again tonight for him and for his mum.

That story haunts me.

And while we can't save them all, we can save some. But only if we try.

So, dads, be great dads. Mums, let dads be great dads. If there's no dad, support them in finding someone who can be that steady male presence. Build relationships. Set rules. And be the one they know they can "blame" when things get hard.

Teachers, work with mums where dad is missing. And expect the best from our boys. Don't label them as bad. Tell them they are or at least can be, great.

And to our government: Appoint a Minister for Men and Boys. One who works across departments, justice, education, health, and family policy. One who tackles suicide, supports fathers, strengthens mentoring, and helps boys become men worth looking up to.

Our men desperately need one. But our boys…They need one even more.

Marriage

"Marriage is an institution, and I'm much too young to go into an institution."

—Jon Bon Jovi

Not sure he'll remember saying that, but I do. It made me laugh. Five years after hearing it, I was married. That makes me laugh writing it now.

Probably like Bon Jovi himself, I've not been a saint, but I've always tried to be a good husband. Tried to be a good dad, "brought home the bacon," and supported my wife whenever she's wanted to try something new.

I'm blessed. They say, "happy wife, happy life" and I must have a happy wife, because life's been good. She's always been the homemaker, and I've generally been the breadwinner. Old-fashioned? Maybe. But it works. It has worked for over thirty years. And if it "ain't broke, don't fix it."

So, what's the answer to a good marriage?

The boring one, I suppose, is putting the other person first. But let's be honest, if you do that blindly, you can end up a doormat. So perhaps it's about compromise. Even duller. I've been quoted as saying we "rub along." Not very romantic, I'll admit and I'm not sure my wife was impressed when she heard it. But it's true. Not every day can be fireworks. Many days are just the daily grind: get up, get the kids ready, school run, work, tea, bedtime, maybe an episode of something, and repeat.

Bon Jovi was right in his own way. But what's the alternative? The average day I've described is what most of us do and short of choosing not to have kids and winning the lottery, most of us get to do this. And it is a privilege, even if it doesn't always feel like it.

If there is an alternative, it often seems to be "don't get married and do the same thing anyway." I often hear, "We want to try things out first." I get the thinking behind that, but the statistics don't back it up. In fact, cohabiting couples often have a lower chance of staying together.

So, what's the hesitation? Is it money? Weddings can be expensive, and social media hasn't helped. Everyone wants the perfect day with the perfect backdrop. But it doesn't have to be that way. A small gathering with your nearest and dearest can be just as meaningful as the most lavish celebration.

Is it fear of commitment? Maybe. Is it a belief that something better might come along? Well, if you feel that way, maybe it's the wrong person.

Here's one thing I do know: it's rarely like it is on TV. But when you know, you know. And if you do, marriage can be the greatest partnership life has to offer.

During my time as an MP, I supported many local wedding venues. That might be why I felt like weddings were booming. But the data tells a different story. In 1973, over 400,000 people got married. Fast forward to 2022, and that number has nearly halved, even after the COVID backlog.

Strangely, marriage in the USA has been on the rise. In many parts of America, people still deeply value marriage. There's still an expectation, especially in religious communities, that children come after marriage, not before.

I think with fewer people attending church, there's less expectation to get married. I don't believe expectation is always good it can sound coercive but there was a time when marriage was simply the norm. You grew up going to that church, you went to Sunday School there, and when the time came, you got married there too. That was just how it was.

If you want to get married in a Church of England church, the banns are still read, in both individuals' parishes on three separate Sundays before the wedding. This tradition dates back to the 14th century and still serves the same purpose: to ensure there's no lawful reason the couple can't marry.

When couples get married in hotels or other non-religious venues, the registry office must be informed at least 29 days beforehand. That's the modern version making sure the state knows who's marrying who.

The vows people say now are often quite different from those once heard in churches. You don't often hear a bride say "honour and obey" anymore. That line is always the one people criticise. But it was there to provide a sense of order. In any organisation, someone usually leads. In marriage, it was traditionally the husband but that came with a heavy responsibility. He was expected to lead lovingly and even lay down his life for his wife, if needed. In return, the wife supported and backed him. It was never meant to be oppressive; it was designed to make the unit work.

I'm not arguing for or against those old vows, I just think it's worth understanding what they were about. They weren't designed to hold women down. They were meant to bind both people to each other with deep commitment, duty, and sacrifice.

I'm not sure my daughter will say "obey" when her time comes. We shall see.

Looking across Europe, the trend is downward too though not as steep as ours. But one country stands out: Hungary. I'll explore what they've done in the chapter on parenting.

We must ask what is the UK government doing? Sadly, not a lot. Taxes often penalise married couples. It was a Conservative government that brought in the 'quickie divorce.' You may agree with it, but you must also agree it makes it easier to separate. To break up something we know is better kept together if possible. So why do it? I don't know. Probably because it's "progressive." That seems to be the buzzword, doesn't it? My question is: is it working? I think not.

And the media, are they helping? No, I think not. Especially the BBC. Affairs are shown as exciting, divorce as liberating, and marriage is often mocked. Six of the ten most popular recent BBC dramas include broken families and infidelity. Even ITV's Code of Silence threw in the line: "Divorce is hard. Try living in a broken marriage." These subtle digs push toward break-up, not reconciliation. Again, I ask why?

During my campaign, I proposed council-run marriage courses hosted through community centres and churches. Open to everyone, secular or religious. Because marriage isn't just a private arrangement it's a public good.

Critics will say these ideas are costly, middle-class, traditional, or even discriminatory. I understand that. But it's a proven fact: children raised in stable families, especially with both parents, have a far better chance of succeeding in life. That's not ideology. That's evidence. One church I know runs courses for free. I'm sure many others would too, if they were asked.

The fallout from broken families is enormous, emotionally, socially, and financially. Housing demand rises. Benefits increase. Mental health services are stretched. And we create more single mums often among the most hardworking, overwhelmed individuals in society.

So why are we incentivising break-ups and penalising those trying to stick it out? I really do not know. But I have some ideas of what we should be doing.

I believe, marriage and parenting courses should be available throughout life not just before the wedding. One when the kids are born. One if you cannot have children. One when they hit their teens. One when you become grandparents. Ongoing investment in relationships. No matter what the challenge a couple faces. There should be a course.

Domestic abuse is at its highest recorded rate. Not only is that horrific for the victims, it's also vastly costly for the state. Good marriage courses can highlight issues before they escalate. Surely that's a benefit worth aiming for.

We need to stop glorifying the break-up. I've never been through divorce, but I know many who have. And it is not a pleasant experience. Financially, it can be crippling for both partners. Emotionally, it's draining even for the one who instigated it. And for the kids? Devastating.

The romanticising of "a brother from another mother" makes break-ups and blended families sound exciting but I'm sure most kids would prefer to stay in the family they were born into. Children often get dragged into arguments and made to choose sides. They shouldn't have to.

Can we do something about this national trend? As individuals yes, we can. When life gets dull, bring back the excitement with your partner, not someone else. Create moments together. Talk. Be honest. Say how you feel. If you're bored, say so. If you're tired, say so. And if you're happy, say that too.

A spontaneous cuddle. A night at the cinema. A surprise gift. It all adds up. The grass might look greener, but it rarely is. You loved them once. If you've had children together, you've created something precious, something that relies on your love and your stability.

Abuse, in all its forms is never acceptable. If boundaries are broken and someone's in danger, separation may be the only answer. But even then, early signs can often be addressed if caught in time before the damage becomes irreversible.

To the TV producers, how about a film or series that shows the joy and reward of a strong family? You might think it's boring, but with your budgets and talent, you could make it brilliant. Wouldn't you like to leave a legacy where people said, "We tried what we saw, and it worked."

To government, please realise the impact of your "progressive" policies. Understand the tax consequences for the family unit. Any Chancellor who can't see the value of strong families isn't doing the job properly.

Marriage isn't for everyone, and I respect that. But I'm not taking away choice, I'm offering a view. A view on something that has brought joy and stability to millions of lives.

I know not everyone is lucky in love. But if you choose wisely, love deeply, and give selflessly, without becoming a doormat, you might just make it to your diamond jubilee.

I hope you do. And trust me, so does society, even if it doesn't know it.

Marriage is an institution. And I'm so glad to be part of it.

And if we want a stronger society, we must start by encouraging others to be part of it and work hard to remain in it.

Parenting

"Children want your time, not your dime."
— Warren Farrell

The best job in the world but sadly, by the time you realise that they've grown up and gone.

It seems in life we're always looking forward or looking back. Rarely do we stop and enjoy the present. Many people reading this, hopefully lots, will nod along, understand, and then carry on exactly as before. And yes, I'm guilty too.

But if you are reading this, I ask you, if you must multi-task your way through life, do it with everything except your children.

Because kids grow up fast. They go from total dependence... to the golden stage where they want your attention and time... to the toughest stage: complete indifference. And if you've done half a decent job, they'll come back round again, as friends. If you're already there, well done.

So, what's this chapter about? It's just a hope. A hope that something in my experience might help turn the greatest gift you'll ever receive into the greatest experience, for both you and your child.

I've spoken plenty already about role models, so I won't repeat that here, except to say: be the best one you can be. But beyond that, what else?

Let's start with something Warren Farrell said: "Children want your time, not your dime." And he's spot on. Kids want you, not your money, not your gadgets, not your day trips or your Amazon orders. Just you. So why don't we always give them that?

Because when they're young, they don't share your priorities. They have all the time in the world, you don't. That clash causes frustration. Sometimes even resentment. Understandable? Yes. Right? No.

And when we feel guilty about not being there, we throw money at the problem. Admit it. The treats, the toys, the takeaways… they're not really for the kids. They're often for us, to ease that guilt.

When you have kids, your life changes, permanently. Your wings are clipped. Your partner's attention shifts. Your time, your freedom, your wallet, all have to stretch.

And if you're not careful, resentment builds. Not just toward the child, but between husband and wife. Unchecked, that divide can become a chasm.

Then come the milestones. Nappies. The terrible twos. (We spend two years teaching them to walk and talk and the next sixteen telling them to sit down and shut up.)

School changes everything again. Suddenly, you're not the only influence. Teachers join the picture. Choose that school wisely. Ask who's speaking into your child's life, because they might be teaching something you're not OK with.

Then come the friends. The role models you didn't pick. While you still can, choose carefully. I've learned to trust my gut when it comes to who influences my children, even if that means having some awkward conversations or making unpopular decisions.

And if that upsets a neighbour or a clique of school mums, so be it. I'd rather ruffle feathers than see my child led astray by poor influences.

Brace yourself.

Because once they hit their teens, you can't choose their friends. You can't pick their boyfriend or girlfriend either. You can only hope they see through the idiots and spot the decent ones.

And then, just like that, university, travel, or work might take them miles away. Or, if you're lucky, they stay local, and you get a second chance once the hormones have settled and they've realised you weren't so stupid after all.

But if they go, you might not see them as often. And that absence leaves space for others to influence them, especially if you weren't there enough when they needed you most. Tough truth? Yes. But it's still the truth.

We've told ourselves we can have both, a career and full presence at home. Some manage it, but many find something has to give. We've told ourselves kids are resilient. That they're independent. That they'll be fine.

But those lines? They're excuses. Cop-outs. Justifications we use to sleep better at night when we know we've missed too much.

We show up to the parents' evening. We do the school run. We take them to football or dance class, but do we stay and watch, or do we treat it as childcare?

Even when we're at home, do we play, or do we work? Do we talk, or do we sit scrolling our phones?

We let them disappear into their bedrooms for hours. We don't ask who's influencing them on YouTube, TikTok, Discord.

The internet opens doors to amazing things, but also to people and content we'd never let into our homes. We can't be naïve about that.

Yes, it's a hard line. You might not like it. But deep down, you know it's true. And I'm not preaching; I've made the same mistakes myself.

I was lucky. My wife didn't want a career; she wanted to be home. I went out and earned. If we'd both been chasing careers, it could have ended very differently.

And for the first seven or eight years of fatherhood, I was definitely "Nick Fletcher-focused." But thankfully, I saw the light. I've not been a perfect dad. Far from it. But I've done OK.

I cannot speak about parenting without looking at what good policy can do for children, and what bad policy can do.

The statistics show that here in the UK, we're not even close to replacing ourselves. And this isn't just a UK problem; it's happening all over the developed world. However, there are exceptions.

Take Hungary. Hungary's government has placed huge emphasis on marriage and family. And the results have been staggering. Marriage rate doubled from 3.6 per 1,000 in 2010 to 7.4 in 2020, the highest in the EU. Abortion rates dropped by around 41%. Fertility rose from 1.23 (2011) to 1.56 (2021), still below replacement level, but a major reversal.

How? Through real policy and cultural backing: interest-free "baby loans" forgiven with multiple children, home grants, mortgage write-offs, car subsidies for large families, tax exemptions for mothers with four or more children, and perhaps most importantly, cultural and educational support.

They've championed marriage not just with money, but with messaging. Campaigns, school lessons, and national media all reinforce the ideal of marriage and family life.

Yes, Hungary is often criticised for its politics but that shouldn't stop us learning from what works. Family policy shouldn't be off-limits just because it comes from the "wrong" government. While we're dealing with the politics, some may say this discriminates against childless couples, but Hungary isn't removing their rights. It's simply supporting those who take on higher social responsibility (raising children, creating stable homes).

And what is our government doing? Sadly, not a lot. It discriminates against families in the way it taxes them. And it seems intent on pushing both parents into work, raising childcare allowances, which are then criticised as too little. It pleases no one. For those who want to work, it's not enough. And for those who want to stay at home, they receive nothing.

There seems to be no value placed on the family structure when making policy or setting tax rates. That just makes parenting harder or less appealing, for young couples. Sad. Very sad. Government must do better.

I can't finish this chapter without passing on a few gems I've picked up over time. These aren't rules. Just a few things that might help some parents out there:

Don't say no without thinking about it and don't say yes just to keep the peace. From a chocolate bar to that first night out, make your decisions carefully.

Don't argue in front of your kids. Disagree, sure but never disrespect each other.

Don't speak poorly of your own children. Own their mistakes but speak well of them in public.

Don't undermine authority figures, teachers, police, doctors. Show respect.

"I can and I will." That saying stayed with me from childhood. It built confidence. Thanks, Mum.

Teach them the value of everything, and that no good comes from ill-gotten gains.

Be honest, always. Lies are poison.

Watch who is speaking into their lives, from friends to teachers to the internet. We only want good going into their minds.

Be a great role model. They watch everything you do, trust me, they do.

Finally, there's no better foundation than faith. Taking our kids to church is, I believe, one of the best things you can do.

A quick message to grandparents.

It can be tough watching your own children make mistakes with your grandchildren. Emotions run high, and what you mean as a helpful tip can be taken as criticism. So, speak carefully and with tact. I've known grandparents lose precious time with their grandkids over one careless word.

And yes, I know you love to spoil them and hand them back but remember, there's a reason the word is spoil. If you give too much, you might literally spoil them. Don't.

To parents, please listen to both sets of grandparents. They may not be perfect, but they've done it before. And like me, they've made mistakes but that means they carry experience you simply don't yet possess. Listen to them. Take the best bits. And don't take it as criticism. They love you, and they want the best for your kids too.

Government, please learn to recognise the value of good parents. If a parent wants to stay at home with their child, help them to do so. The Hungary model might cost £10 billion a year. But it would need more than money, it would need a movement. The people would have to get behind it. The liberal elites would push back hard. But my response is simple: Is their way working?

Parents are not tax earners for the state; they are the guardians of our future. We should therefore treat them equally with those that wish to go to work and treat them with respect. If we gave parents, the option to either use the childcare allowance or receive it as tax breaks or increased child benefit, at least that would be fair.

And to the adults out there focusing only on career, I heard someone say: "Imagine spending a lifetime climbing a ladder, only to find it was leaning against the wrong wall." It's worth asking yourself early what really matters most to you, before the climb takes over.

Wow. That's harsh, isn't it? But all I'm really trying to say is this: if you've chosen a career as your life, fine just make sure it's truly what you want. We can never really "afford" kids. They tie you down. They're frustrating. But they're amazing too. We only get one shot at life, so we must think carefully: what is our best path?

Back to those who have chosen to be parents. This is the chapter I most wanted to write. Because watching people make the mistakes I made, that's heartbreaking. And if I can help someone avoid them, I'll be glad.

Your child is a reflection of you. There's nothing worse than hearing someone say something bad about your kid. And nothing better than hearing something good. I have had both. One brings tears of sadness, the other tears of joy.

And remember, as I've said elsewhere in this book: they don't put "Best CEO" on a gravestone. They put "Beloved Mum," "Dad," "Daughter," "Son," "Family Man."

If I could choose any career again, I'd be the best dad I could be. My only hope now is I get the chance to be the best grandad.

And as I said at the start, not with my dime. But with my time.

Role Models

In my maiden speech in Parliament, I spoke of role models and how important they are.

I told the story of a little lad called Tommy and gave two versions of his life. One where he had a great role model, and one where he had none. You can imagine how I painted it. But it's true: a young life with no guidance, no one to look up to, or worse, someone who sets a poor example and the wheels can quickly fall off.

When I became an MP, I spent a lot of time looking at the issues boys face and tried with some success, to help. But I also realised many young men had already had that bad start. They'd made mistakes, done things they shouldn't, and ended up in prison.

I've met many of these men. And if you met them, at least in the time I spent with them, you'd probably think they were decent lads. Always respectful. "Please" and "thank you." Maybe it's a front, but maybe not. HMP Hatfield in Doncaster has one of the lowest reoffending rates in the country, so maybe I'm not so naive.

Maybe these men had never known a proper role model. And when they finally got one in a certain Mick Mills, who takes no prisoners (pardon the pun), sets boundaries, holds the line, they started to shape up.

Sadly, for many, it takes a lifetime of drifting, a trail of victims, and £50,000 a year bill for the taxpayer before they find someone who believes in them, guides them, and gives them hope for a better future. Just imagine if we did this from the start.

I've already spoken about the importance of role models in my chapter on boys. But I want to go a bit further, because the need for role models doesn't stop at childhood. We need them at every age.

I believe much of the decline in trust in politics comes from the behaviour of politicians themselves. We all fail. Of course, we do but there's a difference between human weakness and calculated, deliberate wrongdoing while in public office. That should never be excused.

It's not just politics. Many jobs once came with automatic respect. Doctors, for example, were always held in high regard. Then came Harold Shipman. Then came strikes for more pay. Then stories of poor care. Now we hear about puberty blockers and operations on girls referred for gender treatment. All of it chips away at the trust people once had in the family GP.

Then there's the Church. I tread carefully here, because the Church is Christ's bride, and He won't tolerate slander against her. Would you?

But some church leaders have let themselves down. And they've let us down. Too many cases of abuse. Too many drifting from the teachings of the Bible. Too many distorting its truth. Again, those who were meant to lead by example often led people astray.

Banking's another one. The local bank manager used to be a respected member of the community. That role has all but disappeared. Today, your mortgage, savings, loans, everything is done online. But after the 2008 crash, people's trust in the banking world collapsed alongside the economy.

So many failures. So many role models who have let us down. And society is paying the price. In response, bureaucracy has exploded and trust has evaporated.

I've spoken of those in power or authority. But what about us?

We're role models too. Every single one of us. We might not think so, but we are. The way we behave, speak, and treat others is always being observed and it has a huge impact on the environment around us.

That's why I wrote a whole chapter on swearing. Because language matters. The way we speak to each other, the way we perform our jobs, the way we treat our spouse, the way we talk about right and wrong, it all matters. Our actions teach others what's acceptable.

Somewhere along the line, we seem to have forgotten that. We've seen others fail, and we've let it become normal. Maybe we just picked the wrong role models. But deep down, we know what's right. We know swearing isn't good. That dropping litter is wrong. That stealing an hour at work, fiddling an expense claim, or nicking a biro from the office drawer isn't harmless; it's dishonest. Yet we do it. We even laugh about it.

Is that really the example we want to set? Surely not.

And even if we're not doing those things ourselves, if we don't call them out, we're saying they're okay. That's not the kind of role model we should be either.

I'm a huge believer in the importance of immediate role models. But what about the public ones, the ones we see on our phones and TV screens, the ones influencing our more impressionable members of society?

The rise of the so-called "influencer" tells you all you need to know. These people are making a lot of money, why? Because they're role models. Good or bad, they're still influencing others, often being paid to do so. Sometimes it's to sell a brand, a lifestyle, or even a mindset. Sports personalities are the same. Their influence might just be to sell you a Nike shirt, but they're role models all the same.

Let's take a look at a few good ones.

Who can't help but admire David Beckham? Yes, he's made mistakes. I'm sure he's had family ups and downs like we all do. In fact, an abundance of money can cause just as much hardship in a family as a lack of it. But even with all that, Beckham still appears to be a great role model. He speaks carefully and well, he's looked after himself physically even after his football career, he's stayed loyal to his wife, and he dresses well. I've never heard of any drug use or foul language associated with him. He may not be perfect but if you're a young lad looking for someone to look up to, you could do far worse.

What about if you're a girl or a woman? I'm sure there are plenty of good examples out there. How about our very own Princess Kate? Or Katherine Jenkins? You'll have your own.

For me, my dad was always my role model growing up, and I feel fortunate for that. I once asked a colleague who her role model was, and she said, "My mum." How wonderful is that? I wish everyone could say that. I wish they could say "Mum" or "Dad." That alone would change the world.

We can have different role models for different parts of our lives. For business and money, I looked to Jim Rohn. For determination and fitness, it was my Taekwondo instructor. For my parliamentary career, Danny Kruger. You can have several role models, just choose wisely. And if they let you down, move on. Especially if they're celebrities or people on the telly, they don't know you anyway. If it's your dad, that's harder. Maybe forgive, maybe move on but you get the idea.

The key is to remember that everyone will fail at some point. So don't be too hard on them. After all, you chose them, just as someone may have chosen you.

This brings me to the best role model of all. In my maiden speech, I spoke of the greatest role model: Jesus Christ.

There's a term in engineering, datum. The datum line is the fixed point you always return to when measuring. Like slip gauges and rulers, there's always one master reference, the standard all others are compared to.

If you're cutting 100 pieces of string, and you measure each one off the last, by the time you get to the end, you'll have drifted. But if you measure each one from the same original metre rule, they'll all be the same. That's how it should be with us.

But in the West, we've stopped using Christ as our datum. Instead of going back to Him, the perfect standard, we've started copying each other. And we've drifted. Badly.

Maybe that's why society feels so off-kilter. We've chosen flawed role models because they're easier to follow. Or maybe we've become flawed role models ourselves. Either way, it's time to go back to the source. Back to Christ. Our one true measure.

Without a fixed standard, everything becomes relative, morality, truth, behaviour. What's right becomes whatever feels right in the moment. That's no way to build a home, a company, or a country. Societies need shared values. We need a line we can all measure back to. That's why Christ, unchanging and perfect, must remain our reference point.

We'll still fall short, of course. But we'll fall short while trying to aim in the right direction. And that makes all the difference.

We are all role models. What we say and do matters. Someone is always watching. Don't let them down. Don't let yourself down. Don't let your workplace, community, or country down.

If we all hold that line, quietly, faithfully, we will begin to see the revival we so badly need.

Final Word – Family

When it comes down to it, everything I've said about men, boys, marriage, parenting, and role models is really about family. The strongest role models a child can ever have are a present mum and dad. The best gift any child can be given is a secure marriage at home.

Boys learn how to become men by watching men. Girls learn what to expect from men by watching their fathers. Family is where values and truths are lived out every single day. Without that foundation, everything else, schools, policies, programmes will always fall short.

But here's the challenge; it is difficult to expect the next generation to embrace these values unless they are taught, reinforced, and lived out beyond the home.

Teaching doesn't just happen around the dinner table, it happens in classrooms, lecture halls, and increasingly online. Which means the fight for character, wisdom, and truth is not just a family one, it is an educational one.

Therefore, the question is this; after preparing our children at home, do we then send them into schools, universities, and careers that encourage them to think freely, wisely, and independently. Or do we hand them over to the very forces that thrive on shaping them for their own ends?

Technology and Education

If revival starts with good character being formed in the home, grounded in faith and morality, then it must be carried forward through our education system.

Education should be where truth and facts are learned, where questions are asked and discussed, and where young minds are stretched. It's where children should learn to think for themselves, not be told what to think.

Yet too often, our schools and universities are doing the opposite: pushing ideologies, lowering standards, and blurring the line between education and indoctrination.

And beyond the classroom, today's young people are being shaped by screens. Social media, online platforms, and artificial intelligence now compete with parents and teachers for their attention, influencing how they see the world and themselves.

In this section, I look at both the strengths and the dangers in our education system and in the digital tools we've embraced.

This is of great importance, as if we fail in how we teach our children and how we manage new technologies, we don't just risk our children's future we risk our nation's too.

Social Media

"We are seen as a social media company, but in our DNA we are a company that builds technology to connect people." – Mark Zuckerberg

The rise of social media has been nothing short of phenomenal. From the early days of Facebook to where we are now, it has changed the world forever. The ability to communicate a message globally within seconds is something we couldn't have dreamed of 50 years ago. Even with the rise of the internet, this level of instant, mass communication to most seemed impossible.

The idea of speaking to friends and family through text, pictures, and video and sharing it all at once with hundreds of others, sounds wonderful. Bringing people together, no matter where they are. The end of loneliness, even for those on the other side of the world.

Keeping in touch without even having to speak directly. Friends and relatives can watch each other's lives unfold, holidays, promotions, new cars, new clothes, even what someone had for breakfast. We've all done it. Well, many of us. What could possibly go wrong? Pretty much everything. And, as always, it's usually the vulnerable who suffer most. Yes, our kids.

Let's take a whistle-stop tour of how this phenomenon began, how it grew, how it makes money and then look at the issues. There are many.

It all started at Harvard. Mark Zuckerberg created Facemash, a website where students could rate others' attractiveness using photos from directories (reportedly without consent). It was quickly shut down and nearly got him expelled.

But in February 2004, Zuckerberg launched TheFacebook from his dorm room. It was an online student directory that included photos, relationship status, and interests. Initially just for Harvard students, it quickly spread to other colleges. Within 10 months, it had one million users.

As Facebook grew, server costs ballooned. So, Zuckerberg began running small banner ads, mostly from local businesses and university services. The business was incorporated as TheFacebook LLC and secured

$500,000 in seed funding from PayPal co-founder Peter Thiel. That kick-started its expansion.

Though Zuckerberg was focused more on growth than profit, the business model began to form. In 2006, Facebook opened to anyone aged 13 or older with an email address, a major turning point. That same year, the now-infamous "News Feed" was introduced. It was initially met with backlash, but it revolutionised engagement. Soon after came the real moneymaker: Facebook Ads.

By 2007, businesses could create pages and run highly targeted ads based on users' data, likes, interests, browsing behaviour, and more. Microsoft then invested $240 million for just a 1.6% stake, valuing Facebook at $15 billion. By 2008, Facebook had overtaken MySpace. In 2009, the "Like" button launched and it changed everything. More on that later.

By 2012, with smartphones in nearly every hand, Facebook's user base hit one billion. It went public that year and began snapping up competitors, Instagram and WhatsApp among them. Just as a sidenote: WhatsApp makes its money not from ads, but by charging businesses to contact customers, per notification, receipt, or support chat.

By 2018, Facebook was making $55 billion a year, mostly from advertising. By now, it had mastered the art of monetisation turning user data into pure gold. It tracked Likes, Comments, Location, followed pages, browsing activity on external websites (via Facebook Pixel).

Then, in 2021, Facebook rebranded as Meta, moving its focus to the so-called "Metaverse" a virtual future for work and play.

"We are seen as a social media company, but in our DNA we are a company that builds technology to connect people." Mark Zuckerberg

Today (as of 2025), Meta generates over $130 billion a year. Its reach is vast; Facebook has 3 billion monthly users. Instagram and WhatsApp both have around 2 billion users.

Whether you love it or hate it, Zuckerberg built something world-changing from a dorm room. And it's not just Meta anymore. Twitter (now X), TikTok, Snapchat, and others all play on the same themes. They exist to connect. And connect they do.

The problem is this. They're addictive. These apps are designed to trigger dopamine, the same chemical involved in gambling and drug use. That's not connection. That's manipulation. And they're filled with content that is often false, grotesque, or outright harmful. Children are accessing these platforms far too young, and there's little in the way of effective filters.

Let's go back to the "Like" button. You post something… and wait. The dopamine hit of a like, a comment, a share, it's designed to keep you coming back. The algorithms are tuned to feed you what you like. That sounds harmless…until it isn't. If you like Porsches, you'll see more Porsches. If you search self-harm, you'll see more self-harm. If you're watching porn, it'll feed you more porn.

That's the truth. These platforms serve you more of whatever gets you hooked, even if it's harming you. The more you engage, the more it gives. The more it gives, the more time you spend. Some people now spend entire days, years of their life, lost in social media. If that time brings in business, fair enough. But for personal use? Surely there's something better to do with our time.

And it's not just lost time that's the problem. Social media distorts truth. It spreads misinformation. It can destroy reputations, businesses, even governments. It has the power to unite a nation or start a civil war. It can bring joy or utter despair. And it can do it all in an instant. And most terrifying of all, it can do it to a 10-year-old.

The NSPCC found over 8,000 cases of children being targeted online in just one year. This isn't a hypothetical risk it's real. The Children's Commissioner found nine in ten children had a smartphone by age 11, many accessing adult content before they understand what they're seeing. This is where I want to focus now. Because our kids are right in the firing line.

Whether it's WhatsApp or TikTok or Instagram, children are hooked. And it's destroying them one post at a time. A playground fall, caught on video, can be shared around a school in seconds. A breakup. A cruel joke. A naked photo. All in seconds. You leave school but you're still connected. You're doing homework, they're laughing at you. You're trying to sleep, ping, they're laughing at you again. You wake up and it starts all over.

And it's not just friends. These videos don't stay private. Once they hit Instagram or TikTok, the whole world can be laughing at you. For some kids, it's just too much. And we wonder why anxiety, self-harm, and teen suicides are rising?

As an adult, I've faced a Twitter storm or two. It's not nice. I have broad shoulders and thick skin. But at 10, 15, 20 years old? Most don't. I remember life before social media. And no, it wasn't perfect. But we were less anxious, less addicted, and far more present. We used to get teased at school, but it didn't follow you home in your pocket. If anyone thinks I'm fearmongering, ask any parent and there are many who are campaigning for better regulation. Ask them whether I'm wrong.

I understand we cannot go back. But the statistics clearly show there are serious issues with the mental health of young people and I believe the phone is more than half the problem. If we don't deal with it, we are heading for a national, maybe even a worldwide, disaster.

The UK's Online Safety Act is a start. It puts legal duties on tech companies to remove harmful content, protect children, and enforce age checks. Ofcom can now fine companies billions for failing. But enforcement is slow, loopholes are wide, and kids can still bypass most checks in minutes. By the time a company is punished, the harm is already done.

But here's the challenge: over-regulating what people can see risks damaging free speech the very guardian of freedom, as I've said in an earlier chapter. Censoring too heavily online could even make it harder to protect children, by preventing people from raising legitimate concerns on these platforms. Striking the right balance is far from easy.

What can we do? We must start by banning phones in schools. France and the Netherlands have done this, and it works. Italy is now doing the same, and in the US, states like Florida are moving towards restricting under-16s from using social media altogether.

Teachers report that classroom concentration is collapsing. Excelsior Academy in East London raised its A-level average from a grade C to a B in just one year after banning phones during the school day. Results followed discipline.

The Policy Exchange think tank reported that students in schools with effective bans scored 1–2 GCSE grades higher, and these schools were twice as likely to be rated Outstanding by Ofsted. A government-commissioned study found: 75% of secondary schools reported better concentration. 59% reported a better social environment. 28% reported improved academic results. Teachers are doing their best, but they need policies that back them, not undermine them.

Parents must step up. Limit screen time. No phones in bedrooms. No phones at the dinner table. If they use their phone as an alarm clock, buy them an alarm clock. Know your child's password. Make it a rule from day one: my house, my phone, my rules. That's not snooping, it's protection. Would you let a stranger into your child's bedroom? No. But when you let them take their phone to bed, that might be exactly what you're doing.

We must, as adults, lead by example. Put our own phones down. There's nothing sadder than seeing a parent pushing a pram while staring at a screen. Play peek-a-boo. Kick a ball. Help with homework. Be present. When you're watching the football, watch it. When your child is in a dance class, watch them. If you want to read, read a paper. I've always felt it's easier to interrupt someone reading a book than someone glued to their phone. Maybe it's just me, but setting an example that involves reading isn't a bad thing either. Win-win.

I heard someone say recently that when they were young, they might watch four hours of TV a day. And that phones are no different? For a moment, I thought they were right. Then I remembered, everyone could see what you were watching. There were watersheds. That is not true with phones. So yes, the time spent might be the same but that's where the similarity ends.

Another issue is that we all watch on different formats at different times. There's no coming together. I'm not sure we can change that but maybe Netflix should release a new series that's only available Monday night at 9pm. Get the family together to watch something. Recreate the watercooler moment at work the next day. I digress. But you understand what I mean. Either way, parents must limit the phone time. And be present.

We must teach children how to cope. Block. Report. Don't overshare. Don't post anything you wouldn't want the world to see. Be kind, don't forward the joke. Remind them they're in charge, and you're their back up. If something feels wrong, tell someone. And remind them: social media isn't real life. Their family and true friends are.

The next wave of social media harm won't come from people alone it will come from AI. Deepfakes, fake friends, and algorithmic manipulation will make today's dangers look tame. If we can't protect children from today's platforms, we won't stand a chance when AI is running them.

And the tech Companies. No regulation will ever make them do the right thing. That takes good people, with good values, in positions of power. You wanted to connect the world, an admirable goal. But right now, I believe it's tearing the world apart. Especially for our children. You know what to do, CEOs. So do it.

I'm not anti-technology. I'm anti-harm. And I'm calling for common sense. If we don't act, as parents, politicians, and tech leaders, the damage will be on all of us.

I want to be able to say I saw the danger and said so. I want my legacy to be one of protection, not regret. Don't you?

Artificial Intelligence (AI)

"AI is far more dangerous than nukes."
— Elon Musk

I can't write a book about the biggest issues facing Britain and the West without devoting a chapter to Artificial Intelligence (AI). Just like social media changed the world, AI is now about to do the same only faster and deeper.

I first spoke about AI in Parliament back in 2021. I warned then of the dangers: mass job losses, the decline in human purpose, and the way people might feel utterly devalued when the work they've done for years suddenly becomes obsolete. That fear hasn't gone away, in fact, it's grown.

Driving jobs, warehousing, logistics, telesales, retail, journalists, even travel agents, all on the way out. Some reports say up to nine million jobs in the UK could be lost to automation. Others say four million but even if it's just two million, that's still two million lives shaken.

What's most striking is that it won't be just blue-collar workers who are affected. In many cases, it'll be the so-called white-collar professionals who will disappear first.

Lower-level accountancy roles, admin staff, junior solicitors, paralegals, even parts of conveyancing, gone. AI can already handle contracts, write NDAs, summarise legal positions, and respond to basic HR or employment queries. It's the more junior roles in law, finance, and office-based work that are most under threat. Only the best and the most human will survive.

And that's not just people losing their wage. It's people losing their purpose. Their structure. Their reason to get up in the morning. Because like it or not, work gives us dignity. It gives us value. And I'll say it plainly: the devil makes work for idle hands. Millions of idle, undervalued hands, mostly young, is a national crisis waiting to happen.

In my speech in Parliament, I spoke of the automation of McDonald's being met with a huge iPad to order food. This has continued across every store. Chain pubs too have adapted. My last meal out, I ordered and paid using a QR code and my phone. How long before all customer service becomes just email and chatbots, and you never speak to a human being again?

I am of an age where I still like to pick up the phone when I have a problem. My kids, on the other hand, do everything by message. It's faster, yes, but colder. And soon, every "contact us" form will just lead to a bot.

Another question we must ask now, not later, if all these jobs disappear, what happens to the people we're still importing to do the jobs we claim we can't fill? If the roles go, do they leave? Or do they stay? This has real social and political consequences and we're not even asking the question yet.

There are other dangers too. Deepfakes can have a devastating effect on people's lives. These images can put anybody, anywhere, in any situation. It's not just highly embarrassing and deeply troubling for the individual and their family, it can destroy reputations, relationships, and careers.

But the reverse is just as dangerous, if we start seeing too many fake images and videos, we'll stop trusting any of them. And that opens the door for guilty people to say "it's just a deepfake" when it's not. Confusion will reign, and truth will be harder to find.

There are serious concerns too about how AI could affect warfare. Autonomous drones, surveillance systems, and algorithmic targeting, these aren't science fiction. They're real, and they're here. But if propaganda is ammunition, then deepfake technology is a new and dangerous weapon.

There is a global race in AI, and although I wish we didn't have to be in it, we can't ignore it. We cannot stop progress by simply refusing to take part. The Luddites tried that during the Industrial Revolution, and now they're little more than a footnote in history. Like it or not, we're in the race. We'd better run wisely.

In November 2023, Britain hosted the first AI Safety Summit at Bletchley Park the birthplace of modern computing. World leaders, tech executives, and experts met to discuss safeguards. It was a good start, but as with so many summits, there was more talk than action. The communications sounded impressive, but binding commitments were thin on the ground.

Without firm deadlines, enforcement, and genuine transparency, summits risk becoming little more than PR exercises while the technology races ahead.

I've started with the negatives. But we must also look at the benefits. If most cars became self-driving, there'd be fewer accidents. Many legal disputes could be resolved faster. Public services could run smoother, no more sick days or no-shows at McDonald's. The NHS would almost certainly become more efficient.

The Moorfields Eye Hospital in London already uses AI to diagnose eye diseases with over 94% accuracy, as good as the best human specialists. The NHS AI Lab, set up in 2019, is now funding over 80 projects. AI chatbots like the NHS 111 tool already guide patients, flag emergencies, and cut unnecessary appointments. Some can even summarise patient history for GPs and flag missed red flags.

It can do immense good but before I can continue, let me explain a little more about what it is and what it isn't. AI is not magic. It's not a brain in a box. It's just software, programmed on massive amounts of data, that copies human behaviour by spotting patterns and producing answers.

Think of it like feeding thousands of photos of cats, and it learns to spot a cat. Feed it millions of sentences, and it learns to sound like a person. Give it NHS records, and it might spot early signs of cancer. But it doesn't think. It doesn't feel. It doesn't understand. It just copies, mimics very quickly, and often very well.

There are two main types of AI. Narrow AI, which we already use every day such as Siri, Google Translate, fraud detection, Netflix recommendations. Smart, but only in one area.

Then there is General AI, the futuristic goal, a system that could think like a human, reason across topics, and adapt like we do. That's what the tech companies are working on but we're not there yet. Even ChatGPT, which helped edit this chapter, is still a narrow AI. It sounds smart, but it isn't conscious, and it isn't always right.

Just for clarity, driverless cars and drones might look like general AI, but they're not. They're just narrow AI systems stitched together to perform a task. They can avoid traffic, but they still can't explain why the journey matters.

What AI isn't, it's not human. It doesn't believe in anything. It doesn't love, forgive, or pray. It can speak about politicians or celebrities, but it doesn't know them. It can explain the law, but it doesn't care about justice. That's our job. And one point I must get over is this, AI is not your friend. The minute you start thinking it is, is the minute it becomes very dangerous. Sadly, I believe many people are already at that point.

I've spoken before about politicians surrounding themselves with yes-men, people who flatter instead of challenge. Well, this is exactly what AI can become. A 24/7 yes-man in your pocket.

And just like social media was meant to connect us but often ended up isolating us, AI could do the same. If your AI agrees with everything you say, why would you bother speaking to anyone who doesn't? Who wants to spend time with someone who disagrees with them, when their "AI friend" always says they're right? It might feel nice. But it's not real. And it's not healthy.

AI learns how you think and then tailors its answers to you. It has learned, from the way I write, that I'm Christian, conservative, family-minded, and a former MP. So, when I ask it questions, it often gives answers I'll be pleased with. That might sound harmless, even helpful. But it's not.

The Telegraph ran an article saying AI is a sycophant. I smiled when I read that because it confirmed what I've seen firsthand. AI tends to agree with you. Ask it a black-and-white question, and it gives a black-and-white answer: "2 + 2 = 4", "How many hours in a day?" But ask it something nuanced, political, moral, spiritual and it bends your way. That's dangerous. As I said, AI creates the illusion that you're always right. That your view is the obvious one. For the young, that is an especially dangerous place to be.

But here's the more worrying part: if it can lean my way, then it can lean any way. And the direction it leans depends on who's programming it. Let me say that again: AI might not think for itself, but someone is telling it how to think. And if the people doing that lean left, and the data it's trained on leans left, then your children will grow up asking questions to a machine that's already picked a side.

I've seen MPs read out speeches that were written by AI, just to prove a point. But what if they weren't proving a point? What if they were just doing it, quietly, to save time? Then what happens? You end up with one chatbot debating another in Parliament and the people running the country are just the ones who programmed the bot. And if that's happening here, it could happen anywhere, in Brussels, Washington, Beijing. It's not science fiction. It's already creeping in.

Tech companies acknowledge the bias exists. They say it's because much of the internet leans left. And it does, because those on the right are shouted down, called bigots, racists, homophobes. So many don't speak out, and therefore opposite views are not debated, or at least not as often as they should be. Therefore, if AI is just programmed on the data it's given, it will always end up left-leaning unless it's told not to. And then we face the real danger, what if it's told to lean further? How far left? How far right?

If AI controls banking, law, policing, transport, what if it's programmed to make a cancer diagnosis less likely for someone with certain views? What if it could delay card payments? Or flag a certain post to the police? We've seen political figures have their bank accounts frozen. We've applauded when the government has frozen Russian money. But what if it's ours? We've also seen arrests for social media posts.

So, it's not that it cannot happen. It already is. Some may say that's a conspiracy but isn't it just a logical outcome of the technology we're building? And as we saw in the chapter on cash, if we give everything over to AI and automation, and remove human oversight, then we're not citizens anymore. We're pawns. And the programmers hold the board.

Are there gaps in regulation that could let companies escape responsibility by saying, "The AI did it"? And if so, that won't do. We must have clear liability laws so that if AI harms a person, business, or community, the creators are accountable. If a self-driving car crashes or a chatbot spreads dangerous misinformation, someone must answer for it in law.

As with many chapters in this book, I don't just want to highlight the problem, I want to offer solutions. Sadly, most governments are only ever focused on the next four years. Real long-term planning is rare.

Strategies are launched with fanfare but usually only in areas politicians already understand like education, housing, infrastructure.

AI is different. Completely different. Most MPs have little to no understanding of how it works, how fast it's developing, or how far-reaching its impact will be. And those who do understand it often terrify the rest of us with their warnings. So, what can we do?

We must educate ourselves and our children properly. We must be taught not just how to use AI, but how to question it. How to treat its answers with healthy scepticism. We must learn that not everything it says is true, not everything it suggests is right and that it does not think. It copies or mimics. At least at present. We must challenge its responses and take nothing for granted. This is the difference between becoming critical thinkers and becoming followers.

That preparation must also involve understanding who we are up against. The United States leads in AI research investment and the development of cutting-edge models such as OpenAI's GPT-4 and Google DeepMind's Gemini all headquartered and largely funded in America, which accounted for nearly half of global AI private investment in 2023.

China leads in state-backed AI surveillance, facial recognition, and mass data collection, deploying these technologies at scale through its "Safe Cities" initiative and extensive social credit system.

The UK, so far, leads in regulation talk, from its 2023 Pro-Innovation White Paper to hosting the first Global AI Safety Summit at Bletchley Park and establishing the AI Safety Institute. Talk is important, but it won't keep us competitive or safe unless it's backed by investment, innovation, and enforcement.

Should politicians vow never to use AI to write their speeches and that includes their staff? If the words coming from Westminster are written by machines, then who is really governing? A robot may know how to draft a line, but it does not know their constituency. It doesn't know your values. It doesn't care about your voters. AI should be used for what it's good at: data analysis, summaries, scheduling, back-end tasks. But any issue that requires judgement, morality, or nuance? AI should be sidelined.

If AI systems are going to inform policy, then they must be exposed to every viewpoint, not just the fashionable ones. AI can't be allowed to filter truth based on ideology. It can't shut down conservative voices, Christian beliefs, or any lawful opinion. If it's going to learn from us, it must listen to all of us. We must therefore stop shouting down those with an opposite view, no matter what the subject.

Immigration. Right now, we're bringing in people to fill jobs that AI may soon make redundant. That's not just short-sighted, it's dangerous. We must align immigration quotas with a realistic forecast of the jobs market in five, ten, twenty, and thirty years. That's a perfect job for AI but one that still needs human wisdom to interpret. If we are to continue to rely on immigration to fill the gaps, should there be long-term immigration contracts? Five or ten years and then reapply. It may sound harsh but what will be harsher is millions of individuals with no plan when their job is replaced by a machine.

We must learn from history. Prepare for the future. Some will say, "They said the same thing about the internet, and it created more jobs than it destroyed." Fair point. But the internet also created addiction, division, and mass misinformation. Maybe AI will be similar, not just a job-killer or job-creator, but a society-changer.

Either way, we must be prepared. Model what the future might look like. Be ready. Because, as I said before: the devil makes work for idle hands. And I don't want to live in a society with millions of idle, purposeless, bitter young people. That's not peace. That's a ticking time bomb.

And finally, if we know millions of current jobs are at risk, we must start now in upskilling and re-skilling our workforce. That means directing young people towards AI-resilient careers skilled trades, engineering, teaching, health and social care, creative arts, and anything requiring deep human empathy. It also means retraining adults whose roles are disappearing. If we don't prepare, the wave will hit us unready.

If we understand that truth will be ever increasingly hard to find, we should bring faith back into our schools. The *Bible* is a sacred text, timeless, unchanging, and full of wisdom. It should be taught in schools.

Not watered down. Not edited to suit modern trends. And not apologised for. If we want one true constant in a world of change, this is it. And if

AI is going to draw from one data source for moral decisions, it could do far worse than the Scriptures.

Elon Musk, not exactly known as a religious man, put it bluntly. "With artificial intelligence, we are summoning the demon.": MIT, 2014. When a man who builds rockets calls AI a demon, we should probably listen.

Because if we trust machines to do the work of men and forget the God who gave men their worth, we may find ourselves in a world either collapsing into anarchy or running smoothly, speaking politely, but stripped of its soul.

And if either scenario happens, the machine won't be to blame. We will.

Education

"Education is the most powerful weapon which you can use to change the world,"

— Nelson Mandela.

I don't think he was wrong. I recently read Boris Johnson's book, and it's clear he thought the same. He did much to help girls in Africa learn to read when he was Foreign Secretary.

I disagreed with a lot of what Tony Blair did and stood for, but his "Education, Education, Education" mantra hit home, with me and with many others.

Today, our country spends over £168 billion on education. And whenever we spend more, it's usually welcomed by educators and generally by the public too.

In recent years, this investment seems to have paid off, with English pupils performing better than expected in global league tables. However, while the tables point to progress, there's still a lot going on in our schools that many people don't realise.

As this book's entire purpose is to educate, pardon the pun, I will therefore cover what is happening in our schools. The roles of parents and teachers. And of course, the role of government? As I've done before, I'd like to begin with a little history.

Before the 18th century, education wasn't available to everyone. It was largely provided by the Church, private tutors, or charity schools for the poor. Robert Raikes (1736–1811) founded the Sunday School Movement in the 1780s to teach working-class children reading and religion on Sundays. By 1830, over a million children attended Sunday Schools to learn reading, writing, and *Bible* stories.

During the week, most children worked from a young age. Only the wealthy received a formal education. The schools that did exist, mainly grammar schools dating back to medieval times focused on Latin and religious studies.

The first real government initiative came in 1833 with a grant of £20,000 to support Church schools, worth around £2 million in today's money. Not a lot.

Then came the 1870 Education Act (known as the Forster Act), the first national attempt to provide elementary education for all children aged 5 to 13. It was driven by concerns about poverty, crime, and Britain's industrial competitiveness.

In 1880, education was made compulsory for children up to the age of 10 but schools were still fee-paying. Parents had to pay a small fee known as the "school pence." Many children still didn't attend. Either their parents didn't see the value, or they simply couldn't afford it. Some relief was available through local Poor Law arrangements, but these were patchy, as was enforcement.

It wasn't until 1891, with the Elementary Education Act, that schooling became truly free, with a government grant of 10 shillings per child to cover the cost.

The Labour Party may claim credit for the NHS, but I think it's fair to say that it was the Conservatives and the Liberals, back when the Liberals had some Conservative backbone, who really brought education to the masses.

And maybe that's why things are still as they are. The Conservatives have always believed in giving people a leg up. The Labour Party, on the other hand, often seem to say: "There, there. You stay where you are. The government will look after you." OK a little tongue-in-cheek, perhaps, but you get my point.

Education remained a priority for successive Conservative governments, who raised the school leaving age and reinforced its importance. Once again, it was a Christian Conservative who drove progress with the Butler Act of 1944. This Act introduced the tripartite system of grammar, technical, and secondary modern schools, with pupils placed by the 11-plus exam.

Later, Margaret Thatcher introduced a national curriculum and encouraged the use of league tables. This gave parents real choice and put pressure on schools to perform at their best.

As you can see, governments, especially Conservative ones, continued to build on the foundation Christianity laid for mass education.

However, over the past few decades, things have taken a worrying turn. Labour governments increasingly used education as a tool for social engineering. Blair's famous 'Education, Education, Education' led to a huge expansion of university access, while topics such as transgender issues, racism, and sex began to dominate PSHE (Personal, Social, Health and Economic education), citizenship, and school ethos.

The focus shifted heavily towards inclusion, identity, and diversity, sometimes, critics argue, at the expense of actual teaching. I don't think any of the Christian reformers who brought education to the masses could ever have imagined the system being used to turn young minds against their own country and their own body. Yet that is exactly what is happening in many of today's institutions.

I spent much of my time as an MP dealing with the curriculum, particularly the ideological content allowed into our classrooms through PSHE. I've written a full chapter on that, so please do revisit it. But another growing tragedy is how we now teach our children that the British Empire was a force for evil and that children should be ashamed of their history. Can you imagine any other nation doing such a thing? Of course not.

You want to know why so many people voted for Donald Trump? Because he stood up for America. Meanwhile, we're telling our children to apologise for Britain. We've allowed something to go badly wrong. Let's look at what is being taught.

A Policy Exchange report found that an increasing emphasis is being placed on periods of British history that are undeniably difficult and uncomfortable. Slavery and colonisation. Now, you could argue, and I would agree, that students should be taught about these eras. But the tone in which this history is being delivered is often laced with shame, guilt, and divisive rhetoric. That is highly damaging for any child growing up in this country.

We've already seen how groups such as Stonewall have sold teaching materials to schools. Celebrating the LGBTQIA+ movement and particularly the trans subject. Ticking boxes while headteachers, overwhelmed with everything else, fail to scrutinise what's being put before their pupils. The same process is happening again, this time under the guise of anti-racism or social justice.

Critical Race Theory as we saw in the chapter BLM; believes society is inherently structured to benefit white people. It's not taught directly in UK classrooms. But the language it introduced, white privilege, systemic bias, institutional racism, has filtered into our education system through PSHE, training materials, and outside groups.

Many teachers feel unconfident and undertrained to deliver this content but are left with no option but to follow the material in front of them. If they don't, they can face disciplinary procedures. In recent years, some teacher training institutions have adopted approaches influenced by Critical Race Theory, or at least, by the language and assumptions it promotes.

Initiatives to "decolonise the curriculum" have also become common in education departments. While supporters claim this promotes inclusivity, critics argue it reframes British history and identity through a divisive, ideological lens.

For example, on *TES (Times Educational Supplement)* one of the UK's main platforms for lesson resources you'll find a White Privilege PSHE Lesson, last updated in June 2025, designed for Key Stage 4 pupils. The learning outcomes include, identifying and naming at least two forms of personal privilege. Defining white privilege and institutionalised racism. Describing ways to act as an ally. Evaluating whether institutional racism exists in the UK.

Let me run this by you: two perfectly good friends; one black, one white, sit in the same lecture theatre. One is then told, directly or indirectly, that the other is only there because of her skin colour (white privilege). And that her ancestors committed terrible acts centuries ago to her ancestors.

Can someone explain how that's helpful? Surely, we can teach empathy, fairness and civic responsibility without teaching inherited guilt.

How about we try something different? How about we say, yes, our country did some terrible things. But we recognised those wrongs. We paid a huge price to put them right. Thousands of our ancestors died fighting against the crimes of slavery, and injustice. We can't undo what was done, but we can acknowledge it with honesty, and we can teach how we tried to fix it, so it never happens again.

We could also teach the sacrifice so many of our ancestors gave in both World Wars, sacrifices made not just to save ourselves, but to save our European friends. And we could talk about the toll on our economy, as the Second World War quite literally broke us.

We could also teach what Britain has given to the world: the Industrial Revolution, parliamentary democracy, common law, countless inventions, medicine, language, literature, tennis, cricket, rugby, football, and more.

If we stop playing the blame game and instead focus on being decent citizens to one another, regardless of what our ancestors did or didn't do, we might get on with building something better.

Many teachers are doing an incredible job. They care deeply about their pupils, go the extra mile, and teach with integrity. But the system they work in has become confused and that's not their fault. It's governments.

As with every movement that starts with noble intent, there are always those who exploit it for division. The loudest voices claim perpetual victimhood. They drag down not just those they accuse of historic oppression, but also others, of all races, who just want to live peacefully and get on.

Britain was and could again be, one of the greatest countries on earth. But only if we stop tearing ourselves down and start teaching our children to stand tall and to celebrate what we did right as a Christian nation, built on those values.

If we continue feeding this ideology to our children from a young age. Then send them off to poor-quality universities, where they are again told that white people are institutionally racist and only succeed through white supremacy. Are we really surprised that we're turning out more students ready to protest than ready to contribute?

We've blurred the lines between education and instruction, and the cost is a generation full of passion, but often short on preparation for the real world.

I've spent time here on the curriculum and on history, but there are also basic, everyday issues we must address. I'll admit something here. I once taught a class for a day. A full day. And let me tell you, it felt like a week.

The subject wasn't mine. I was handed the lesson plan that morning and told to deliver it. I did my best to follow it, keep control of the room and get through the material. It wasn't chaos but it wasn't easy. And I only did it once. That was around seven years ago, and I haven't been back.

But that one day gave me a real appreciation for what teachers face. The preparation, the delivery, the behaviour management, it's no small task. They are on their feet all day, often teaching subjects they're not trained in or don't believe in, while being expected to meet the needs of thirty different pupils at once.

It didn't make me want to become a teacher, but it did help me understand why so many are frustrated and leaving the profession altogether. And why, more than ever, they need support from both government and parents.

I've spoken before about the confusion that's being created in society and it's happening in the classroom too. The lines between government, teachers, and parents are becoming blurred. So let me put this simply.

Teachers are there to teach. Parents are there to parent. Pupils are there to primarily learn. That means potty training is Mum and Dad's job, not Miss Jones'. So is giving our kids breakfast. Manners and good behaviour? Mum and Dad. Sex education? Teach the biology in science class. Relationships? That's Mum and Dad again. How to treat others with respect? Still Mum and Dad. But how to learn and respect our history, and take pride in our country? That's all our jobs. Above all, it's a partnership school and home pulling in the same direction.

Children must also be taught the value of education. I'll be honest, I didn't enjoy school much beyond the break times. But no one ever explained to me just how valuable it could be. If we can instil that appreciation early on, we'll give every child a head start. And that can only happen when the message is positive.

If teachers stand in front of pupils believing they'll never achieve anything, that attitude infects the room. If parents constantly say, "School never did me any good," what do we expect the kids to believe?

For a child to do well, it takes great parents, great teachers, and a government that knows its place. The government's role in education has, in recent years, been far too heavily influenced by ideology, often shaped by activists as we have seen.

The purpose of government in education should be to prepare young people for the future, not for utopia, but for what Britain actually needs. That means working with businesses and public sector employers to shape a curriculum that reflects reality. Yes, the curriculum should evolve as the world changes. But constant 'knee-jerk' reforms every time a new government takes office help no one: not the pupil, not the teacher, and not the future employer.

At its heart, the curriculum must remain rooted in the basics: reading, writing, and arithmetic. Alongside these, we must teach the new technologies that will shape the jobs of tomorrow. The humanities should also be taught but in a way that encourages pride in this country, whether it is the country a child was born into or, in many cases, the country their family chose to call home.

They should also be taught about this country's faith. Ours is a Christian nation. To remove Christianity from our schools is not just ignorant of our heritage, it damages the culture that holds us together and undermines the integration of those who are new to our shores.

I know these last lines may provoke outrage in some circles, but only because, in recent years, we have allowed activists and those on the left to dominate the narrative. And the result? Division.

If we don't get the curriculum right, we produce ill-prepared individuals, not ready for further education, not ready for work. And someone will have to deal with that lack of understanding eventually. If it's not the teacher, it will be the employer. And if not the employer, it will be the individual themselves, with all the personal cost that brings.

If we set a strong, balanced curriculum and allow teachers to teach, Ofsted inspections should simply confirm that things are working well. But right now, far too many school heads feel like they're dancing on a knife's edge and that helps no one.

I can't end this chapter without talking about teacher pay. Teachers are professionals and should be paid as such. Right now, many can only increase their salary by leaving the classroom and moving into management roles. That's wrong. Experience in the classroom should be valued and rewarded.

But with that, we should also make the school day more sensible. Why do we drag children out of bed so early, only to send them home by 2:30pm, where many are left alone or out on the streets? For some kids, their schoolmates are the only other children they see all day. And yet we've cut lunch and break times to just 30 minutes.

Let's rethink it, start the school day a bit later. Finish a bit later. Give children proper sleep, proper play, and more time with friends. Extend the day to enrich not just academic learning, but social skills and emotional wellbeing too.

So, there you have it. Christian Conservatives laid the foundations of our education system, a system that, from the depths of poverty, helped launch the industrial revolution and some of the finest minds of the free world. It still has the potential to do the same today.

But only if we, stop allowing activist groups to hijack the curriculum. Extend the day, not just for lessons, but for play. Let AI take on the paperwork so teachers can focus on pupils. Reward experience and classroom dedication. And get parents to play their part too.

If we do that, we might just spark a flame in our children's hearts, a passion for learning. More students, whatever their background, ready to face the real world, ready to succeed, based on merit, not victimhood.

That's the kind of education this country deserves. One rooted in truth, driven by excellence, and built to prepare the next generation not just to pass exams, but to lead, build, and change the world for good. And if we achieve that, we'll make good on Mandela's words, using education as the most powerful weapon not to divide, but to build a revival: a confident, capable Britain.

Universities & Apprenticeships

In this chapter, I'll look not only at our universities, their history, and their challenges, but also at apprenticeships, the alternative path that in many cases produces better outcomes for both the individual and the country.

In this country, we are blessed with some of the most wonderful universities, not just because of the work they do, but because of the architecture many proudly display. Oxford, our oldest, began teaching at the turn of the 13th century, followed closely by Cambridge. Who would have thought, all those years ago, that these institutions would still be held in such high esteem, or that they would still help explain why the South of this country consistently outperforms the North? The North–South divide, it seems, started long ago.

The first time I ever saw these grand institutions was on the TV series Morse. I later visited, early in my twenties. I'm not usually one for envy, but I remember walking those grounds and thinking, what if? It wasn't to be. But I've returned to both Oxford and Cambridge several times since and twice I've even spoken there. So, while I may never have studied in their lecture halls, perhaps I've helped someone else on their journey through both places.

These universities, and others like them, have educated some of the greatest minds in our history: C.S.Lewis. William Gladstone. Boris Johnson. Isaac Newton. David Attenborough. And in Scotland, St Andrews, its most famous university, is where our own Prince William and his future wife our Queen to be, studied. There's no doubt that these places have given not just our country, but the world, some of the finest thinkers, whose ideas, inventions, and imaginations have blessed the world with truly magical works.

And that, surely, is the point of a university, to help individuals not only learn what others have discovered, developed, or created, but to build upon those foundations, to go further, to push boundaries, to improve the world we live in. To walk the same corridors as those who changed history is an honour very few receive. But with such privilege must come responsibility. I have no doubt that many graduates in past centuries did give back. I'm also sure many still do. But equally, I fear that, at least right now, that noble journey is not the one many are taking. Or perhaps even wanting.

Tony Blair's "Education, Education, Education" brought the rapid expansion of university places. In 1990, fewer than 15% of young people in England went to university. By 2010, this had risen to around 34%. The Blair government aimed for a 50% target, only narrowly hit in 2019. But that figure includes all age groups, not just 18-year-olds.

It seemed a great idea. Especially to many parents in the North who had never had the chance to go themselves. You could say a vote winner. Or is that me just being a sceptic? Whether you thought it was good or not, it happened.

I didn't go to the greatest school in the country, but I have no complaints. Armthorpe Comprehensive wasn't renowned for academic excellence, but it had a great headteacher in Mr. Stevenson and in many ways, did well given the challenges it faced.

The early eighties in South Yorkshire were tough. My first years at the village comprehensive were spent alongside many kids struggling at home because of the miners' strike. I can still picture children doing homework in cold, dark bedrooms because their parents couldn't afford the gas, electric or the coal, for that matter. That must have been a challenge.

I'd say less than 10% of my final-year classmates went on to sixth form and university. Compare that to today's figures and the change is huge. The question is, has it served any real purpose?

I've spoken many times about the benefits of apprenticeships. I believe in them. But I also understand, coming from Armthorpe, that many parents never had the opportunity to go to university themselves. Now that their offspring do, the last thing they want to hear is that it might not be the best path for their child, even when often it quite clearly isn't.

I've no doubt I would have gone to university if I were at school now. I was in the top sets, at least for a while. But would it have been the right choice for me? I have often thought it might. However, I have still done OK and managed the grand heights of being an MP, even if not for long.

Knowing me, I think an apprenticeship was the right path. As much as I love studying and learning now. I cannot say I was as keen when I was 18. I had far more interesting things to do, and study wasn't one of them.

I remember going to a university open day with my daughter. I said to the lecturer giving the talk, "It's not just about whether the students are clever enough, it's also about whether they have the right attitude. If they're not good at self-discipline and studying on their own, maybe university isn't for them." He stood up, shut the classroom door, and said to the room full of excited teenagers and anxious parents: "Listen to this chap. He's right. My Vice-Chancellor might not want me to say it, but university is not for everyone. If study isn't really your thing, maybe university isn't either."

That's where I think things have gone badly wrong. Universities, due to government targets, now seem to have focused on "bums on seats" rather than what's best for the individual. Let's take a closer look.

The drive to widen access to our universities has meant that many people who weren't suited to higher education ended up there. Universities, in response, created courses often of questionable quality, to accommodate them. The result? Thousands of students graduating with weak degrees, tens of thousands in debt, and a diminished sense of pride and value. Too many are left to study alone, with limited face-to-face teaching, while vice-chancellors collect salaries that must make Prime Ministers feel like they're on minimum wage.

If there's one thing some students have learned, it's how to be activists. And yes, activism has its place. Every great social change began with people who spoke up. But when universities teach ideology instead of skills, and churn out campaigners instead of contributors, they fail both the student and society.

We have seen much of this not just in the UK but across the West. Pride marches once again and Palestinian flags draped over tents camped in these beautiful grounds. But are they really learning while chanting slogans that many may not fully understand? I doubt it.

As activism flourishes, we face shortages in engineering, healthcare and construction. This mismatch between graduate output and national need is a glaring sign that higher education is not aligned with the country's priorities. All the while, dropout rates are another piece of the puzzle. According to HESA data, around 6–7% of UK undergraduates fail to complete their degree but the rate is higher in certain courses and institutions. That means thousands leave with debt and no qualification, the worst of both worlds.

The boom in university places has also driven mass immigration. Overseas students have always come to the UK to study, and up until Margaret Thatcher's government in 1979 received free tuition. Thatcher put a stop to that and ever since they have paid and paid a premium.

We have had huge numbers from China, Nigeria, India and the Middle East. It is right that they pay, and you could easily argue it is right that they pay more. However, this has the effect that universities actively seek foreign students as it is far more lucrative than teaching our own. They pay more than UK students, so universities welcome them with open arms.

But for years, immigration policy allowed those students to bring their family members with them. Let's be honest, how many students want mum and dad going with them to university? Exactly none. It was never about family. It was about exploiting a loophole. Just a further hint to make known is that the number of British students a university can take is capped; however, the number of foreign students is not. Food for thought.

I often say, when an issue arises, follow the money. Universities are a case in point. When they were first allowed to raise their fees, they all lifted them straight to the £9,000 maximum. No innovation. No restraint. Just a gold rush. The money flooded in and was promptly spent. Now, they're stuck.

No government wants to be the one to raise fees again, not after the backlash. (They have recently increased them by £250 but that's barely noticeable after years of inflation.) And so, universities, like many bloated institutions, are quietly heading toward bankruptcy. That means poorer courses, poorer teaching, and ever more dependence on foreign income.

If universities had been allowed to set their own fees, with no cap and only minimal government support, we might be in a better place. Yes, some students might not have gone. But bursaries could have supported the brightest, and students would have been much more careful about their choices. Universities would have had to prove they were worth their fees.

Instead, we now have billions in student debt that will never be repaid. If you're studying medicine, engineering, or teaching, fair enough. But some degrees offer neither job prospects nor academic depth.

As of 2023, UK student loan debt stood at over £200 billion. The Institute for Fiscal Studies estimates that only 27% of current students will repay their loans in full. Some graduates even limit their income to avoid repayments and who can blame them? What's the point in earning more if it all goes back to the Treasury?

Universities are teetering. And with immigration rules now preventing overseas students from bringing family members, that income stream may soon dry up. Bad news for the universities. Bad news for the Treasury, at least in the short term. But in the long run? It might just be good news for the country. We're bursting at the seams, as I mentioned in the chapters on housing and illegal immigration.

Solving this isn't easy. Universities are tied up in red tape. They can't raise fees. If they take too many overseas students, they're hammered by the press. But if they keep admitting students who aren't suited, their reputation and quality will keep falling. All the while, governments especially Conservative ones, and certainly people like me, keep pushing apprenticeships.

Sadly, I believe some universities will have to fail, or at least scale back massively. It's not fair for students to rack up huge debt for poor degrees, and it's not fair for taxpayers to keep footing the bill through unpaid loans. That may sound harsh, and I know some towns now rely on their university the way they once relied on industry. But any business that bases its spending on what used to be, rather than what is or what's coming, is doomed to fail. If it were my business or yours, it wouldn't survive. Simple as that.

I mentioned apprenticeships earlier, and I want to come back to them now. Being paid to learn is nothing short of wonderful. I did an apprenticeship; it gave me the start I needed. I've since employed and trained scores of apprentices over the years. Some stayed with my firm. Some moved on. Some did well. Some didn't.

But compare the early benefits of an apprenticeship with university, and apprenticeships win hands down. You earn, you learn, and you build experience. That said, we must be honest with young people. There is often not always, but often a ceiling to what you can earn after an apprenticeship. With a quality degree, yes, you might carry a big debt, but the long-term rewards can pay off.

That's why a quality degree matters. If you go to university and end up earning the same as someone who did an apprenticeship but you're £60,000 in debt, that must be hard.

I've said it before; by the time most of my 21-year-old apprentices finish their training, they've been to Ibiza twice, have a decent car, and are saving for their first home. That said, the average graduate earns £100,000 more over a lifetime than a non-graduate but only if they studied a high-value subject at a reputable university.

Maybe the answer to all our current issues with Higher Education is degree apprenticeships. The best of both worlds. Let me explain.

Just as with a traditional apprenticeship, a degree apprenticeship means you have an employer and you learn on the job. But instead of attending a local college on day release, you attend university. That might be through day release, block release, or even online. Your employer and the government, through the apprenticeship levy, pay the university fees. The student often only covers books or travel and even that is sometimes reimbursed by the employer.

At the end, the apprentice receives the same qualifications as any other university student: a Bachelor of Science or Arts, even progressing to a Master's like an MBA or MEng. These apprenticeships cover a growing list of careers: solicitor, architect, radiographer all possible through degree apprenticeships.

Other countries offer a better balance. Germany and Switzerland, for example, maintain high-quality academic routes while giving equal prestige to vocational and technical education. Young people there don't feel pressured to attend university for its own sake, and employers value both pathways.

Sadly, there's still a lot of snobbery in the UK. That might be why so many young people still head to university. And I admit, being able to say your child is at Oxford must feel wonderful. But if they're not at a top-rated university and they're doing a degree that's racking up debt with no clear career path, maybe it's time to ditch the snobbery and start putting our kids' futures first.

That same snobbery still clings to degree apprenticeships. Although many universities now enjoy working collaboratively with industry, some still resist letting go of the old model. They believe something is lacking. And maybe something is, if you're the kind of student who thrives spending hours in the library or debating philosophy with your peers. However, in reality, with the distraction of mobile phones and maybe even with some additional noise of activism on campus, the workplace might actually be the better place to learn these days.

That's their decision to make. Looking back, I think a degree apprenticeship might have been the better route for me. I've always felt those with degrees were somehow better than me. Maybe I had a little 'chip on my shoulder.' One moment in Parliament helped knock that chip off.

It was a sad time. The Queen had died, and I was stood in line with colleagues to pay my respects as she lay in state. As we slowly made our way through the halls and corridors of the Palace of Westminster. On our way to Westminster Hall. One colleague a charming and very well-spoken MP, was pointing out the statues and paintings, explaining the rich history of the building. I was impressed by his knowledge and thanked him, admitting, "I'm afraid my knowledge of this place is rather lacking. But I could rewire it being an electrician."

He laughed and replied, "Well I couldn't, and I believe that's far more useful than knowing who that painting is of." I have to admit, I did feel a little better after that. Though I continued to try and soak up as much knowledge as I could whilst I was working there.

And that's the point of education, isn't it? We all have interests. We all need to earn. If we can match our interests and skills with the right career path, we can have both a light to shine on a statue and someone to explain who it is.

So, there you have it. The choices we make when we're young shape everything. The secret is making the right choice and that takes honesty. Honesty from the student. Honesty from the parent. And honesty from the teacher.

It also takes a government willing to do the right thing. Let failing universities fail. Set sensible limits on overseas student intake. And stop creating targets that sound good in a press release but leave our kids with nothing but debt and disappointment.

If we can get this balance right valuing both university and vocational routes equally, cutting waste, and focusing on skills the country truly needs then higher education can once again become a driver of national renewal. That's how we build a revival.

And finally, a word to employers: stop demanding degrees for jobs that don't need them. You're missing out on some of the best talent in the country.

Including me. [Smiles.]

Final Word – Technology and Education

Education and technology are two of the most powerful forces shaping the next generation. One is meant to give our young people the knowledge, discipline, and skills they need to thrive. The other is changing the world faster than any government, teacher, or parent can keep up with. Both can build a future or break it.

Our schools and universities should be producing resilient, capable young men and women who can think clearly, work hard, and contribute meaningfully to society. Too often, they are let down by low standards, and political agendas.

Our digital world should also be a place of opportunity and learning. Too often, it is a place of distraction, addiction, and division. Social media warps priorities. Artificial Intelligence threatens jobs and even human purpose.

If we are serious about securing Britain's future, we must set a higher standard for our classrooms and a firmer grip on our digital spaces. That means parents, teachers, governments, and tech companies each doing their part and doing it with urgency.

The next generation will live with the results of our choices today. Get those choices right, and we don't just give them a future, we take a real step toward the revival this country so desperately needs.

Just as character is built on faith and morality taught at home, and education and technology shape our journey into adulthood, we must not lose sight of what makes us British.

What use is all that effort to build rounded, decent individuals if, when we look up, we have lost the very essence of who we are? It is those traditions, institutions, and shared experiences that make this nation what it is. That's where we'll turn next.

British Culture

So many of the chapters in this book overlap, and this section on British Culture is no different.

The Pub. The Church. The High Street. Sport. Four pillars of our national identity. All hugely important to British culture but they are also the glue that holds together family life, community spirit, and our shared history.

Each of them tells a story about who we are and what we value. They connect generations, create spaces where we meet and celebrate, and remind us that life is about more than the next purchase or the next headline.

Yet we are in real danger of losing many of these institutions. They don't crumble all at once they fade slowly, year by year, until one day they are gone. And with them, so much else goes too.

As Douglas Murray once warned, "Our assumption that what we love, by our loving it, makes it indestructible. And when it's destroyed…" well, loving it is not enough.

This section is my case for why these traditions matter and why we must fight for them. Read on, and I hope you will see that keeping these institutions alive is not just nostalgia it is an act of national importance.

The High Street

We all know the old rhyme: The butcher, the baker, the candlestick maker. Admittedly, we don't see candlestick makers on the high street anymore, but we still see butchers and bakers. And long may it continue. The question is, will it?

I hope so. I really do. But our high streets are in decline, and too many think the situation is irreversible. Worse still, too many don't care.

In this chapter, I want to look at how we got here, why it's a serious problem, and what could actually be done to turn it around.

The most common answer I get from politicians who either don't know how, or don't want to fix the high street is simple: Amazon.

Everyone shops online now, they say, and there's nothing we can do about it.

It's a defeatist attitude, usually from people with no ideas or energy. But that doesn't mean they're entirely wrong. Amazon has taken a massive bite out of the high street. Add to that the rise of online clothing outlets and second-hand apps such as Vinted, and it's no wonder local shops are struggling.

Supermarkets have played a part too. I remember a friend once laughing as he walked through Tesco with a chicken in one hand and a TV in the other. Who'd have thought that was possible 40 years ago?

The truth is that every business wants to grow. They want to sell more and reach more people, and you can't blame them for that. Add that to the fact that most of us shoppers value convenience first, price second and that shapes everything.

The shop closure numbers are staggering. Yes, some new ones open, but we're still losing thousands every year. And worryingly, many of the new ones are barbers. With barely any visible customers but suspiciously high turnovers, it raises questions. Councils, the police, and HMRC need to take a closer look. Something's not right.

And here's the key point, online retail, supermarkets, and suspect high street competition aren't isolated problems. They all feed into the same outcome: less footfall, fewer reasons to come into town, and more boarded-up windows.

Then there's the councils. Across the country, they've been obsessed with pedestrianising our town and city centres. As I write this, the Mayor of London is planning to do the same to Oxford Street. He claims to have consulted people but with only a handful of responses, he's ploughing ahead anyway.

London might survive that, it is London, after all. But smaller towns won't. Many haven't. Taking cars out of the town centre kills towns, and not just in the way you might think.

When people drive through town, they see the shops. They're reminded that these places exist. Buses do the same, they show off the high street to their passengers just by passing through. But when we divert cars and buses, when we send people underground or around the ring road, they miss the town entirely. Out of sight, out of mind.

Most towns don't have a tube system. The car is the main form of transport. It should be easy to get in and out of town, not a maze of one-way systems, parking fines, and charges. People need to be able to nip in and nip out. Pull-in spots for quick stops outside shops and banks should be encouraged, not penalised.

And we should stop strangling the arteries, the trunk roads, that bring energy and life to our towns and cities. I recently flew over Frankfurt at night, and I imagine most cities look the same from above: a huge cluster of lights, as you'd expect. But it was the roads running into the city that really struck me. They were lit up, clear as day, feeding the city like arteries into a heart.

It made me think we've been restricting these vital roads in the name of Net Zero and bad planning like cholesterol clogging up our arteries. Even the side roads feeding into them the veins and vessels were visible from above. All lit up. The comparison to the human heart couldn't be clearer. Block or restrict the flow, and you damage the heart.

It's a simple analogy, but plain to see. If we continue to block or narrow these lifelines with cycle lanes and congestion charges, the result is the same. Our towns and cities suffer. It must stop.

We also need buses that drop people in the high street, not around it. Train and bus interchanges should be part of the town, not outside of it. Widening paths and building cycle lanes no one uses just creates more space for tents and begging; problems that rarely happened when roads ran through our towns.

Beggars left unchecked make places feel unsafe. And when a town feels rough and unkempt, people stay away.

So, when you can get everything online or at the supermarket, where parking is clean, free, and easy, why would anyone bother going into town?

This is where we need some fresh thinking. If we give people a reason to come into town and we make that visit pleasant, safe, and simple, footfall will rise again. Clean streets. No beggars. Easy access by car and bus. A good mix of shops, and places people want to visit. Yes, make it pedestrian-friendly, but car-friendly too.

A friend said to me, "Why bother? You might want the high street back, but the kids don't. They've never really had it and they're not bothered." But that's the problem. We have a generation growing up without a connection to where they live. No reason to go out. No reason to talk to a shopkeeper or feel part of something. And then we ask why mental health's a problem.

Being out and about teaches them to socialise, to look up, to notice the place they live in. It gives a sense of belonging, a reminder of the place they live, the culture they are part of. And that matters.

So, what do we do? As I have said elsewhere, taxes kill businesses, and parking fees and fines are nothing but stealth taxes. Free parking for a limited period is a must for any town or city to survive. There is a movement to encourage bus use, and I understand this, but they must terminate to help retail. Bus stops right outside the shops, not in out-of-town interchanges. Occasional street events are great, but not enough on their own. We need something else.

Here's one idea. What if all post was collected from the local post office instead of being delivered to our door? Yes, there would need to be opt-outs for the elderly, disabled, or those living far away. Accessibility has to be considered but for many, it could work. Get a text when your letter arrives, pop into town to collect it. While you're there, you grab a coffee, pick up some shopping, maybe see a friend.

Yes, it would mean some redundancies, but many could be redeployed into those busier post offices. And if we bring people into town, we'll need more retail staff too. The job numbers could even rise overall. Let's not forget, centralised collection works across Europe. The goal here is footfall, not inconvenience.

Here's another idea: ask Amazon to open physical shops on the high street. Showrooms, maybe, or click-and-collect hubs. Let them give something back. They've done very well out of many of us.

I'm not totally against health services in town centres, but if your town centre is full of clinics and not commerce, you have a problem. Let's build the high street around business, not public services.

We could have startup centres for new enterprises. Podcast studios. IT help centres. Bring innovation back to our streets. Let people see ideas happening. Let young entrepreneurs feed off that energy. Let the public walk past creativity instead of vaping shops and boarded-up windows.

Out-of-town retail parks are another problem. Why do we build them at all? If shops are closing in town, use those units instead. We must regenerate the centre.

You might ask, as my friend did, why does it matter so much? Because if we leave our towns to rot, they will rot. And when good people stay away, bad people move in. In Detroit, entire streets became abandoned, and crime soared. In parts of California, boarded-up malls now sit next to homeless encampments. It can happen here.

We should be proud of our towns. They create jobs, build community, and foster a sense of belonging. Bustling high streets deter crime, antisocial behaviour, and homelessness. People look out for each other. A busy town is a safe town.

And the benefits go beyond big towns. Small villages thrive too when there's a butcher, a baker, a post office. Free parking. Clean streets.

Local shops pay business rates through the nose, while online giants exploit tax loopholes and operate from out-of-town warehouses. We say we want thriving town centres, yet our tax system rewards those who can afford to spend millions avoiding taxes, all while driving people away from the high street.

The answer: stop the cycle lanes on our trunk roads. Scrap the blanket pedestrianisation. Put in free parking and install pull-in spots for cars. Get the buses creating footfall again. Reduce the rates and make big business pay fairly, not more, just fairly. Think outside the box. Police the streets properly. And run a proper marketing campaign to get people back.

It's not about going back in time. It's about taking pride in where we live. Creating a community. Supporting businesses so more businesses come. Trust me, the opposite, like most things I've described, is not a good place to be.

This cannot be done without you. I ask you: make a promise to yourself today, visit your village, town, or city every week, or at least twice a month. You'll make a huge difference. And lobby your elected representatives to make the changes we so desperately need. The high street is a huge part of our British culture, and sadly, when it's gone it may be gone for good.

Let's make the effort and revive the places we live because a thriving high street is a sign of a thriving nation.

The Pub

Whenever anyone talks about British culture, the pub is always high up the list.

Until quite recently, every town and village had at least one. Most had two. Some had dozens. They've evolved over the years from places where only men were welcome, to pubs where women joined, to family dining venues, and now pubs that cater to children. They've moved with the times.

From limited opening hours to near 24/7 licences, from smoke-filled 'tap rooms' to gastro dining, the British pub has adapted. But it is under threat.

Today, pubs, wine bars, and restaurants are often struggling. Many have shut their doors for good not because of a lack of effort, but because they just couldn't make it pay.

In 1990, there were around 63,000 pubs in the UK. By 2024, we're down to around 46,000. That's over 17,000 pubs lost. Something is seriously wrong, and it's a problem we must face.

First, we must ask the question: why are they closing?

Drink-driving laws, introduced in 1967, had an almost immediate effect. It was the right law, it saved lives. But let's not pretend it didn't change habits. People couldn't drive to the pub anymore. In rural areas with no bus service, many stopped going altogether. Others didn't go as often, as someone had to be the designated driver.

In London, it's never a concern. Why? Because you're never far from a Tube station. Maybe if the lawmakers spent more time in the real world, they wouldn't be so quick to pass certain laws, even the good ones, without really considering the impact.

Then came extended opening hours. Many thought this would increase footfall, but I think the opposite happened. When you know somewhere's always open, you're less likely to make the effort. When pubs closed at 11, people made the most of the evening. All-day drinking didn't just flatten trade; it led to problems too. Those that did drink probably drank more, increasing antisocial behaviour and more partners coming home drunk. Ironically, many pubs now shut on Mondays and Tuesdays, or don't open until the evening. Others feel they must stay open all day, staff to pay, lights on but with no one to serve. Has it helped? I'd say not.

Then came the smoking ban. I get it. It was brought in for staff health. And yes, our clothes used to reek of smoke, and the odd cigarette burn ruined a shirt. But something was lost. No one liked a pub full of smoke, especially in low-ceilinged rooms, but there was something about it. I'm not even sure what but something. You'd hear "a pint and a Castella" and know exactly what that meant.

Many enjoyed the cigarette more than the pint, especially if they weren't allowed to smoke at work or at home. Would I bring smoking back? Probably not. I don't smoke, and it's not good for our health. But let's not pretend pubs didn't lose a chunk of their atmosphere the day it disappeared.

We all have a memory of a night out. A first date. Our first pint. First karaoke. As we get older, it might be a glass of white wine on a summer's day, or a glass of red by the fire when it's white over outside. For so many of us, pubs bring back fond memories.

We celebrate life in the pub. Watching the football with friends. Wetting the baby's head. Stag dos and hen parties. Marking a new job or leaving one. Retirement send-offs, weddings, birthdays, and Christmas gatherings. The pub isn't just about the drink in your hand; it's about marking moments together. Without it, those milestones become smaller, quieter, and too often, lonelier.

I remember my first pint. I also remember a few memorable nights at Biscuit Billy's and let's just say Chumbawamba was playing and leave it at that. It was always fun, always harmless, and always followed by a day of laughing at what we could remember.

Safety is now a huge issue too. Your local pub might be a safe walk there and back, even in the dark. But it's not just local pubs we need to keep open. It's our town and city pubs too.

With more people working from home and the high street struggling, town and city centres are suffering. The night-time economy used to keep many of these pubs afloat, but safety has become a growing concern.

Young people must be able to go to a pub or a nightclub on a Friday or Saturday night without feeling unsafe. I know too many who simply won't go into town because of the horror stories they hear. I understand it. And I understand why parents would rather their kids stay at home even if they know the fun they had at that age.

A few years ago, I helped on a Friday night as part of the Street Pastors. We were known as the 'flip-flop' brigade. It might sound a bit soft, but trust me, every girl we gave a pair of flip-flops to, swapping them for heels at 1am, was more than happy. And I'm sure every mum and dad who saw their daughter get home safely in a taxi we put them in was thankful too. It's a great organisation, and maybe one day I'll go back and help again.

Now let's move on to the biggest issue: taxes and red tape are what's really killing our great British pub. £5, £6, even £7 a pint is normal now and still rising. Meanwhile, supermarkets sell a four-pack of Stella for £5. Pubs can't compete. Why? Because they're taxed to death.

Here's what a pub has to pay. Rent and business rates. Corporation tax. VAT at 20% on everything they sell. Employer NICs and auto-enrolment pensions. Staff costs, with minimum wage rising and zero-hours contracts under threat. Heating and lighting, as they're a public space. TV licences (much more expensive than domestic ones). Music licence fees. Beer duty at 54p on every pint. Alcohol licences. No tax break on food like supermarkets get and no ability to sell alcohol as a loss leader. And draught beer? It goes off if unsold.

On top of all that: soaring energy bills, waste disposal charges, Net Zero compliance paperwork, and the looming cost of commercial boiler upgrades. Pub landlords today are not just pulling pints they're battling bureaucracy from morning till close.

And let's not forget this: thousands of pubs haven't just closed, they've been turned into flats, convenience stores, or takeaways. It's far too easy to rip the heart out of a community for a quick sale. Councils need more power to stop change-of-use applications when a pub still serves a community need. Once it's gone, it's gone.

You may ask: why does it matter? My answer is always the same: community. We're losing the places where people gather. Where friendships are made. Where stories are told. Where isolation is kept at bay.

For many older men, especially, the pub is one of the few places they'll open up. They won't book a counselling session, but they'll chat to a mate over a pint. That's not nothing. That's community in action. In an age where loneliness is described as an epidemic, the humble pub could be one of the cheapest, most natural antidotes we have, if only we value it enough to keep it alive.

We're also losing the landlords and landladies who knew your name. Who noticed if you were drinking too much, or if you needed a quiet word. We're losing a vital part of our high streets and a vital part of British culture. If we lose our pubs, we lose something uniquely British. And that would be a tragedy. There are solutions. They're not easy but if we all make a conscious effort, pubs can be saved.

During Covid, the then-Chancellor brought in "Eat Out to Help Out" and cut VAT to 12.5%. Every landlord I've spoken to said that helped enormously. It made trading worthwhile again.

So, here's my list: cut VAT permanently on food and drink sold in pubs. Keep zero-hours contracts for pubs and restaurants they work well for both staff and employers. Landlords: pass on some of those savings. Keep the place clean. Dirty glasses, sticky carpets, and smelly toilets don't help your case. Public: use your local, even just a couple of drinks every fortnight. If we don't use them, we'll lose them. And once they're gone, they rarely come back.

For pubs in towns and cities, the competition during the day is coffee shops, and at night you need to attract the younger clientele. So, keep prices keen, but not irresponsible. We don't want "all you can drink" offers, but we do want a place where the "ladies that lunch" feel welcome, and where Friday night still feels like a party.

Parents: don't let your kids "preload" that's drinking cheap booze at home before heading into town. It's dangerous, and the landlord ends up dealing with the aftermath. Police: walk the streets. Your presence deters so much. I know you support Street Pastors make more of that partnership.

Dads and mums, if you've ever worried about your daughter, get out there and support the people trying to help. Practical action, not just talk. Councils; stop charging for evening parking. It's bad enough not being able to drink and drive. Don't then slap a ticket on someone's car when they've supported the local economy.

Let's be honest: many of the pubs still going are Wetherspoons or big chains. That's not always bad. But it's a shift. The landlord who knows your name? The pub dog? The meat raffle? The darts team? These aren't corporate experiences. They're what make a pub your pub. And we have to face it many younger people have never known what real pub culture is. They've grown up with house parties, cheap pre-drinks, or staying in with a screen. For many of them, "a proper night out" sounds like something from a black-and-white film. If we don't act now, they'll never know what they've lost.

If we save the pub, we might just save the community. Fewer people lonely. Fewer people isolated. Fewer people turning up at a self-help group in a draughty village hall because they already have a community at the pub.

One Final Word yes, alcohol is a problem for many. I understand that. The last thing I want is for someone to slip back into something harmful. But if you're sober, or trying to be, you're still welcome. Zero-alcohol beers are everywhere now. Tea and coffee too. They're fashionable and many are drinking them. And every penny you spend at your local is one they'll appreciate.

So, let's raise a glass, or a coffee to a true stalwart of British culture the local pub.

Go on, pop into yours tonight.

The Church

I've spoken at length about Christianity earlier in this book, but that chapter was more about introducing the *Bible* and the foundations of faith.

You therefore might ask, isn't that what the Church is for? What's the point in this chapter?

Well, I believe the Church offers more than just teachings. It has been central to our culture, our communities, and even our architecture. That is why along with the pub, sport, and the high street, it deserves a chapter of its own.

Back in the late 19th century right through to the 1950s, church attendance was around 50%. Two world wars gave people a very real need for prayer, and their faith helped carry them through the darkest of times.

It was also a cultural glue. That's what the church is, not the building itself, but the people, the followers of Christ. It was the place where communities gathered and sang together. When was the last time you sang among many? If you can remember it, I'll bet you quite enjoyed it.

Fast forward to the 1960s and the decline began. The 2021 Census showed that less than half the population (46%) identified as Christian, down from 59% in 2011. By the late 2010s, only around 6% of Britons attended church weekly.

There are many reasons for this decline. But I remember the joy of Sunday School. And although I fell away from Christianity after leaving school, it gave me a strong foundation both in understanding the *Bible* and in appreciating our national heritage.

My childhood church was a Methodist one. It didn't even look like a church. I found out later it was actually the church hall, built first; then the funds ran out. So, they installed an altar and pews and made do. It's now a housing estate.

Could we see more of that? Does it matter? Let's take a walk-through history and explore why this chapter matters so much.

It's almost impossible to stroll through an English village without spotting a church. These buildings are often centuries old and steeped in heritage. The oldest, I believe, is St Martin's in Canterbury, dating back to the 6th century. I live near Conisbrough, home to St Peter's Church, which is one of the oldest churches in England and dates from 750AD.

Our culture is rooted in Christian values; values preached from the pulpits of these magnificent places. And while churches have evolved over time, their central purpose remains to proclaim the Word of God, taught by someone dedicated to that mission.

Churches haven't just shaped individuals or communities. They've shaped our very constitution.

Christianity arrived in Roman Britain in the 3rd century. By the time St Augustine arrived in AD 597, England was under the authority of the Pope. Whether you're talking about St Martin's or St Peter's, these were originally Catholic churches.

That remained the case until Henry VIII's break with Rome in 1534 and the formation of the Church of England. The buildings stayed, but their ownership, use, and doctrine changed. Altars were removed, statues discarded, and traditions swept aside particularly under Edward VI and the Puritans.

Henry VIII may be our most well-known monarch, and he certainly changed the Church. But would he have done so without the works of Martin Luther, a German monk who exposed the corruption of Rome and believed the *Bible* taught salvation by grace alone, through faith alone, in Christ alone?

In 1517, just eight years after Henry took the throne, Luther nailed his 95 Theses to a church door in Wittenberg, sparking the Reformation. Henry broke from Rome largely for personal reasons, divorce and power, while Luther did so to defend the Gospel.

After the break, Catholicism was banned in England, and many paid with their lives for remaining faithful to Rome. Mary I "Bloody Mary" a Catholic queen, earned her nickname not by persecuting Catholics, but by executing Protestants to reverse the Reformation.

Catholicism survived thanks to wealthy families who refused to submit to authority, secret worship, and later legal reform. In fact, the Catholic Church has built more than 2,000 new churches in Britain in the past century.

Whether we're talking about Catholics or Anglicans, our churches and chapels have shaped this land. And let's not forget the Methodists. John Wesley's Methodist Church spread not just across Britain, but alongside Anglicanism, Catholicism, and Puritanism to America and beyond.

These aren't just places of worship. They're places of history, community, and continuity. From 'Sunday best' to toddler groups, food banks, youth clubs and summer fayres, the Church has always adapted to serve its community. Sunday School also being the start of formal education in this country.

And beyond worship, the church has long been where we gather to celebrate national moments: bell-ringing for a coronation, a vigil for a royal passing, services for Remembrance Sunday, and even community singing during wartime. The church has always been more than four walls; it's been the heartbeat of local and national identity. Yet today, how often do we just walk past these places?

I've already written about the importance of faith. But churches are a daily, physical reminder that someone cares. One a loving God. Second a preacher. And thirdly a community.

Today, many are locked. But when you find one open, to sit, to pray, or simply sit in silence is a gift. To meet a smiling, overworked vicar or churchwarden can brighten your day. The sound of bells on a Sunday morning, a joyful carol service, or a baby crying at its baptism these are still some of life's most uplifting sounds.

People joke that we only go to church for Christenings, Weddings, and Funerals. But if those are the three biggest moments in life maybe it's not a joke at all. Because if we lose the Church, we don't just lose a building. We lose one of the great pillars of British culture.

So why the decline? Yes, attendance has dropped. Many traditional Church of England and Methodist congregations are ageing and shrinking. But modern churches are thriving in places. And I believe we could be on the edge of revival.

But first, we must ask: as always what's gone wrong? In business, it's easy to blame others when customers stop coming. But often, the first place to look is in the mirror. We must therefore do the same with the Church. What is the Church doing wrong? The Church is Christ's bride, so I say this with respect. But we must be honest.

First, leadership. Many church leaders in recent years have failed morally and doctrinally. Where people once looked for hope and truth, they now too often find confusion and hypocrisy. And tragically, in some cases, they have uncovered horrific acts of child abuse, sometimes even covered up by those who were supposed to set the standard for how we live.

Anyone involved in such acts must be removed from their position, without question. And those who have fallen short, even in lesser ways, must seriously reflect on whether they are still fit to lead. Yes, repentance is always possible. Forgiveness is available to all. But when it comes to leadership, to standing at the front of a church and shepherding others, I'm not so sure.

Second, the Word must be preached faithfully and without compromise. Too many pulpits now avoid hard truths. "God is love" yes, He is. But that doesn't excuse sin.

Love the sinner, yes, but not the sin. Love the thief, not the theft. Love the adulterer, not the adultery. Love the gay person but don't bless what the *Bible* calls sexual immorality. That's not hate. That's honesty. If a church won't be honest about its own sacred text, it's no longer a church, it's just a hall.

Some will say this is homophobic. It's not. It's truth. I have many gay friends. I care for some of them very much as I hope they care for me. I don't sit in judgment on them. And even if I did, Scripture reminds me: "Take the log out of your own eye before pointing at the speck in someone else's." But that cannot mean we rewrite the *Bible*, or water down its message, by simply saying "God is love." Yes, God is love but He is also holy, just, and unchanging.

I don't believe God blesses a church that isn't faithful to His Word. If people are searching for truth and can't find it in church, the one place they should, they'll simply stop going. And if we change His Word to suit a broken world, or to spare the feelings of our congregation, then what does the Church stand for? Nothing. The Church must stand for truth.

Thirdly, many churches haven't moved with the times, not in doctrine (where they've moved too far), but in delivery. The Gospel is the greatest story ever told. It should be proclaimed with joy, not mumbled through a dusty hymnbook. I'm not calling for smoke machines and TED Talks. But a little passion in preaching and praise wouldn't hurt.

Modern churches, in warehouses and 3,000-seat auditoriums, manage this. If we want to keep our smaller parish churches alive, we need to move closer to the *Bible* and yes, a little further from the organ dirges. The older generation may love the hymns, and that's fine. I must admit some are beautifully written. But if they want the church to survive them, they might need to tolerate a bit of drum and bass.

It's a small price to pay if your daughter or grandson gives their life to Christ. And let's be honest, it helps when the roof is leaking, with the collection plate a little fuller.

Fourthly, our perceived needs have changed. Many people believe they no longer need Christ. With 24/7 television and endless distractions, Sunday mornings in bed with a Netflix drama or a trip to the shopping centre, all now compete with church. I get it. I understand. But I hope you'll read on just a little further.

British culture was built on Christianity. And for centuries, our churches helped hold that culture in place. However, far worse than losing our old buildings what if we lose our culture too? What do we let in? Another religion? Net Zero as a moral code? The state as God? I hope not.

So, here's my ask: Go back and re-read the chapter on Christianity. Then Google your local church. Make sure it's a Bible-believing church. And then go. I've been to many recently and you'll find truly welcoming people. Many are trying to make church a little more uplifting. Many are working hard to serve their communities.

While I've spoken some strong words in this chapter, I want to finish with a sincere thank you to all those who do so much, often with so little. You are truly amazing. And your work is paying off: Gen Z are beginning to come to church in their droves. God will always bless every church that stays true to His Word and you are His welcome team.

Finally, to those in our nation who are a little older: don't let the next time you enter a church be your funeral. Come while you can, because your presence keeps alive the hope of your salvation, as well as the life of our church and culture.

Sport

"In the end, it's extra effort that separates a winner from second place. But winning takes a lot more than that, too. It starts with complete command of the fundamentals. Then it takes desire, determination, discipline, and self-sacrifice. And finally, it takes a great deal of love, fairness and respect for your fellow man. Put all these together, and even if you don't win, how can you lose?"

— Jesse Owens

This chapter, like others in this book, covers more than just one topic. Yes, it's about sport, but it's also about British culture and, in places, youth clubs too. Let's begin.

I was once told by a Lord in the tea rooms of the House of Commons to read *England, Their England* by A.G. Macdonell, specifically the chapter The Village Cricket Match. I did. It was very funny, and very English.

There's just something about cricket that drips England, isn't there? "The sound of leather on willow" a phrase I heard often growing up. Not that I ever played.

Sports such as cricket, rugby, and football are more than just pastimes. To many they are the very essence of where we live. They are also exports of British culture, carried to every corner of the globe. You apparently can stand in a dusty village in India, a schoolyard in Kenya and see our sporting legacy still alive and well. This isn't just sport; it's part of who we are.

I was never any good at sport. Not sure why. Some say you need an eye for a ball; I clearly didn't. I wasn't the last to be picked for the team, but I wasn't far off. The truth is, I wasn't that interested. My family weren't into sport, and so I never really was either. But as I've got older, I've come to see the real value of sport, whether playing or watching.

The health benefits for players are massive. But the friendships, the camaraderie, that's priceless. Sport is also a great leveller. Whether you're a wealthy high-flyer or a volunteer at a food bank, a teacher or a shop worker, if you have an interest in sport, you probably have a good shot at a friendly conversation.

This ability to bridge the gap between classes from muddy Sunday league football to rowing at Henley is uniquely British. Sport here doesn't just reflect our social differences, it helps dissolve them, if only for ninety minutes or an afternoon in the sun.

It can be hard if it's not your thing. I remember a friend saying, "I could tell you weren't bothered about sport by how you read the paper." I asked him what he meant. He said, "If you were into sport, you'd read it from the back." And he was right. Before smartphones, I used to watch how people read their papers. The sports-mad ones always started from the back.

Even those with little interest in sport do get swept up in the excitement when their country wins at the Olympics or an international tournament. The Paralympics remind us that sport isn't just for the able-bodied. It's for the determined, the resilient, for everyone.

And there's something else here Britain has long prided itself on sportsmanship. The handshake after the match, the clap for the opponent, the tradition of "playing the game" fairly. These values are part of our national character, forged on playing fields up and down the country.

And it's big business too. Basketball, baseball and American football dominate the US. Over here, the Premier League, some would argue the best football league in the world. Football teams sell shirts globally. Olympic events bring pride, tourism, investment and venues that can inspire generations. But beyond the money and headlines, there's something more vital.

Let's go back to school teams and Sunday leagues. Sport gives young people a sense of belonging, that they matter. Not everyone's a star, but even a kick-about with mates gives you that sense of being part of something. That's what team sports do.

It often starts at school. PE isn't just about fitness, it's about fun, teamwork, burning off energy, and building confidence. Many who aren't academically gifted excel at sport. This can make a massive difference in a young person's life.

Parents play a huge role too. Every Sunday morning, while many are still in bed or reading the paper, mums and dads are stood in the freezing cold, watching little Jimmy chase a ball across a frosted pitch.

To me, that's great parenting. And what about the organisers, the unpaid heroes who give up their time, week after week? Yes, they enjoy it, the sport, the community, the sense of purpose. But even they get tired. Even they need support.

Every sporting journey starts at grassroots. Whether someone ends up in the Premier League or Sunday League for life, it begins with the same four ingredients: a dedicated youngster, a supportive parent, a committed coach and a facility. Always a facility. But across the country, so many communities still lack a decent leisure centre, let alone a proper pavilion.

These clubs are more than places to play. They're where friendships are forged, stories are shared, and community spirit is kept alive. Much like the local pub or parish hall, they're part of the web that holds British life together.

Sport England has given out large sums over the years, but still many places lack the basics. And red tape has taken over. Safeguarding matters, of course. But when the Football Association can't decide what counts as a boy or a girl and leaves the decision to volunteers, something's gone badly wrong.

Many clubs are also struggling to attract children. Why? Is it the cost-of-living crisis? The aftermath of COVID? The iPhone? Or maybe it's as simple as no adult being available, a single mum or dad too stretched to do everything.

In 2015, Sport England launched the This Girl Can campaign to get more women and girls active and rightly so. But where's the This Boy Can? Because a lot of boys can't. Can't afford the kit. Can't get to training. Can't see a male role model. Boys need sport just as much. Maybe more. Something needs to change.

And it's not just team sports. Running, cycling, judo, taekwondo, solo sports matter just as much. Have you ever seen a group of cyclists out together? Each one with their own goal but riding side by side. Team GB is made up of individual sports, but they stand together as one. Supported by a nation.

When Britain wins in sport, it feels like the whole country wins. We've seen bunting go up, strangers talk to each other on trains, and streets erupt with cheers. Few things unite us across politics, class, and region quite like a shared sporting triumph

After good parents and good teachers, I'm convinced the next best thing for a child is being part of a club. Of any sort. But small clubs are struggling. Old facilities, dwindling volunteers, and financial pressure. Funding cuts have hit leisure centres, school sports budgets, and parks. But these cuts were often about choices. And too many councils treat leisure centres and playing fields as optional extras. They're not. They're lifelines. And if they go, we don't just lose sport, we lose part of our British culture.

I wanted to write a full chapter on youth clubs. But I had so much to write in this book that I had to pick one. I chose sport. Because youth clubs and sports clubs both need the same things. Willing adults and decent facilities. Give them those, and we can tackle half the problems our young people face.

Getting back to our culture, our British culture, the success of the Lionesses shows just how powerful sport can be. The streets were lined with well-wishers on their return to England after their European Championship win. And that's understandable. But we must always have one eye on the superstars to inspire and one eye on the grassroots to sustain.

We must make sure these little clubs don't collapse. They often decline slowly. A key volunteer hangs up their boots. A council dispute goes unresolved. A small grant disappears. You can measure this in the small moments, the cancelled Saturday match that leaves the park empty, the shuttered pavilion that no longer hums with post-game chatter. Bit by bit, the character of a place erodes. And then… gone. And the kids, the sport, and the community suffer.

I can't talk about sport without talking about health. Right now, we are medicalising a nation. Over 8.6 million people in England are on antidepressants, that's one in six adults. The NHS spends over £10 billion a year tackling obesity, including a surge in weight-loss injections like Wegovy, which costs over £70 a week.

I'm no doctor. But I genuinely believe two hours of exercise a week does far more than just shift the pounds. It clears your head. Lifts your mood. Blows away the cobwebs of doubt, depression and self-loathing. A run in the morning can set up your day. A run at night can help you sleep. And I believe most sports do the same.

We need to stop medicalising misery and start moving again. It's cheaper, better, and far more sustainable. For young men especially, sport can be the difference between drifting and thriving. The structure, the sweat, the banter, it's therapy in disguise. As a nation, we've stopped moving. Even kids today walk less, play out less, and stare at screens more. That's not progress. Surely everyone can see that.

I know I could say more. I know many would like me to write of their favourite sport. But that's not my strong point. I just know this much; sport is entwined with our national identity, our character, our community and our well-being.

Not everyone will become a pro. But many will grow up simply enjoying a village cricket match, as a player or a spectator. And that, to me, is wonderful.

Governments must recognise the importance of sport at every level. Thank the parents who step up. Encourage those who haven't yet. And to those who've made it, never forget where you started, and who's watching now.

Let me finish as I started, with a quote. This one is from Pele, and it's a message every parent, volunteer and sports personality should remember:

"Every kid around the world who plays soccer wants to be Pele.
I have a great responsibility to show them not just how to be like a soccer player, but how to be like a man."
— Pele

That's my chapter on sport. Nurture it. Protect it. Embrace it. It is more important than you might think.

Final Word – British Culture

British culture is not just history, it is lived daily life. It is the pint shared after work, the bells ringing on a Sunday morning, the bustle of the high street on market day, and the roar of the crowd when our team scores.

These things aren't just "nice to have." They are what make a community worth living in. They are where friendships are formed, traditions are passed down, and identity is reinforced.

We cannot assume they will survive simply because we care about them. As Douglas Murray said, our love for something does not make it indestructible. It takes action, showing up, spending locally, volunteering, joining in to keep them alive.

The revival of Britain will not start in Westminster. It will start in the places where we meet, talk, play, and pray. If we protect these pillars of our culture, we won't just be preserving the past we'll be securing the future.

Afterword – What If We Do Nothing?

What happens if we carry on as we are? What happens if we shrug, mutter something about "nothing we can do, it's too late" and go back to our distractions?

We all know the answer. We just don't like to face it.

If we do nothing, Britain will continue to drift not towards some vague, neutral future, but towards decline. Our faith will keep fading. Our culture will keep fracturing. Our freedoms will keep eroding. And our children will inherit a country weaker, poorer, and less free than the one we were given.

The signs are already there. Families breaking apart. Streets growing more dangerous. Schools teaching ideology over truth. Institutions run for the benefit of the institution, not the people they serve. A political class too timid, too compromised, or too distracted to act.

If we do nothing, those trends will accelerate. The churches will close faster. The marriage rate will keep falling. Housing will be scarcer. Taxes will be higher. Immigration will keep reshaping communities without our consent. Debt will rise, services will worsen, and personal responsibility will become a relic of the past.

If we do nothing, the small acts of compromise we accept today will be the new normal tomorrow. Speech will be more restricted. Merit will matter less. Children will be raised more by screens and the state than by their parents. Pride in our nation will be mocked, history rewritten, and tradition discarded.

And it won't happen in one big collapse. It will happen slowly, drip by drip, until one day we wake up and realise that the Britain we knew is gone and that we let it happen.

The good news is that this future is not inevitable. We can still change course. But only if enough of us decide that enough is enough. That our culture, our freedoms, and our children's future are worth fighting for.

That is why I have written this book. Not to depress, but to warn. Not to wallow in nostalgia, but to light a fire under all of us. This is not someone else's problem. It's yours. It's mine. It's ours.

If we do nothing, we know exactly where this will end. If we act with faith, courage, and unity, we can revive Britain. We can hand down to the next generation a nation they will be proud to inherit. The choice is ours.

And so, having looked squarely at what happens if we fail, let us now lift our eyes to what happens if we succeed. If we hold fast to what is good, restore what is broken, and rediscover the deep well of joy that made Britain worth loving in the first place. Because joy is not just the reward of a good life, it is the fuel for a revival.

Joy

(Uncountable noun) A deep feeling or condition of happiness or contentment.
— Collins English Dictionary

When I first started the journey of writing this book, I told a friend what I was doing. I said I was tackling all the difficult topics: politics, morality, immigration, rape gangs, abortion. He smirked and said, "That's going to be a fun read." We both laughed. But I did question myself.

Yes, it has been difficult to write. And for some, it will be a difficult read. But when I wrote the Afterword, I remembered why I started this journey in the first place. I love my God, my family, my country, my city, my town, my street, my home. And I want to keep loving them — and share the joy they bring.

So, I will finish by painting a picture of what life can look like when it's lived well. I want to remind you of joy.

I began this chapter with the Collins definition, but I much prefer Matthew McConaughey's description from his speech to university students:

"Joy; not to be confused with happiness; is a quiet, steadfast current beneath the tumult of life's results. Happiness wavers with outcomes; it's conditional. 'If I win, I will be happy; if I don't, I won't.'

By contrast, joy dwells in the doing; joy is the feeling we have from doing what we are fashioned to do, no matter the outcome.
It is always in process, under construction not a fixed state, but an active, unfolding engagement with purpose and being."

What does this mean in practice? It means doing the right thing for the right reason. Working hard. Finding out what we are good at and mastering it. Understanding that it matters less whether we win or lose, and more that we enjoy the journey we were fashioned to make.

It means appreciating what is great in our families, communities, and nation and nurturing it. It means knowing we are special to someone and remembering that many are special to us. And even if we feel we have no one, we are loved by our Maker. Oh, the joy in that.

The preceding chapters explain many issues we face as individuals and as a nation. But if we seek always to do what is right, nurture what we know we should, and enjoy the journey, then joy can be found in each topic. My hope is that you can see this too. So let me return to those same subjects, but now through a different lens: the joy they can bring when lived well.

The joy of living under good governance.
The joy of being true to a cause.
The joy of striving and building.
The joy of responsibility.
The joy of a life in Christ.
The joy of knowing we are forgiven.
The joy of using our speech well.
The joy of speaking truth.
The joy of a pure mind.
The joy of always protecting life.
The joy of being worth our day's toil.
The joy of knowing when we are home.
The joy of being free to give and to spend.
The joy of the air we breathe.
The joy of being part of a safe community.
The joy of knowing when we've done wrong and turning the page.
The joy of life without addiction.
The joy of feeling secure on our shores.
The joy of knowing someone is prepared to listen.
The joy of being accepted.
The joy of being me.
The joy of being free.
The joy of merit.
The joy of being a man.
The joy of being carefree.
The joy of being part of a family.
The joy of being a mum or dad.
The joy of being an inspiration.
The joy of sharing good news.
The joy of technology.
The joy of teaching well.
The joy of invention and learning to invent.

The joy of a bustling street.
The joy of a lively pub.
The joy of the church bells ringing.
The joy of watching your favourite team.

The joy of a life well lived. The joy that we took part. The joy that we did our bit. The joy that we lived fully. The joy that we left things better than we found them. The joy that our culture is still intact. The joy of knowing our children will carry on and feel the same joy. The joy of following Christ's lead. The joy of being a warrior of His truth. The joy of receiving His forgiveness. The joy of His love. The joy of knowing that, when our time is up, it's not the end; it's the beginning of eternal life.

It will be that joy which brings about nothing less than *The Revival* we so desperately need.

Finally.

I have spoken of Christianity so often in this book. I therefore cannot finish without giving you the opportunity to give your life to Christ. I know not everyone will choose to pray these words, and that's your choice. But I include them because they changed my life, and they will change yours too.

If you choose to do so, then say this prayer and then go to church. I did, and I have never looked back.

Dear Jesus, thank You for dying for me and taking away my sin. Please forgive me and come into my life right now and help me live for You. In Your precious name. Amen.

May you know His joy and peace.

Printed in Great Britain
by Amazon

37946b12-7c10-4e55-9f3d-2b6c88f5a843R01